Pieces of Earth

Pieces of Earth
The Politics of Land-Grabbing in Kashmir

PEER GHULAM NABI SUHAIL

OXFORD
UNIVERSITY PRESS

OXFORD
UNIVERSITY PRESS

Oxford University Press is a department of the University of Oxford.
It furthers the University's objective of excellence in research, scholarship,
and education by publishing worldwide. Oxford is a registered trademark of
Oxford University Press in the UK and in certain other countries.

Published in India by
Oxford University Press
2/11 Ground Floor, Ansari Road, Daryaganj, New Delhi 110 002, India

ISBN-13: 978-0-19-947761-6
ISBN-10: 0-19-947761-2

Typeset in Adobe Jenson Pro 10.5/13
by Tranistics Data Technologies, New Delhi 110 044
Printed in India by Rakmo Press, New Delhi 110 020

For my Mother
In memory of my father Peer Ghulam Mohammad

Contents

Tables, Maps, and Figures

Tables

Maps

Figures

Abbreviations

BJP	Bharatiya Janata Party
COHD	College of Humanities and Development
CSC	Cabinet Sub-Committee
FDI	Foreign Direct Investment
HCC	Hindustan Construction Company
HEP	Hydroelectricity Project
IWT	Indus Water Treaty
KHEP	Kishanganga Hydroelectricity Project
LoC	Line of Control
MoU	Memorandum of Understanding
MW	megawatt
NGO	non-governmental organization
NHPC	National Hydroelectric Power Corporation
NRLD	National Register of Large Dams
PSU	Public Sector Undertaking
PDP	Peoples' Democratic Party
SP	Superintendent of Police

Acknowledgements

No scholarly work is possible to accomplish without the support of people, who directly or indirectly contribute to the process of research. This work too is the outcome of the support I have received from many academics, friends, and well-wishers. Equally important, is the contribution of the respondents in Badwan, Khopri (Bandipora), and Srinagar in the state of Jammu and Kashmir. I am indebted to all these people for not only spending time with me, explaining the processes and impacts of land-grabs but also inviting me for meals often.

The intellectual seeds of this work were sown during the critical development studies course that I took in my PhD, at College of Humanities and Development (COHD), China Agricultural University. I hugely benefitted from the classroom discussions and lectures that were delivered by Henry Bernstein, Saturnino ('Jun') M. Borras Jr., and Jennifer Franco at COHD. Jun Borras, Jennifer Franco, and Henry Bernstein would often push me to look at different dimensions of land-grabs. I would like to thank all these people for their support and critical feedback. Jennifer Franco read some portions of an early version of this book and gave her feedback.

This book would not have been possible without the scholarly guidance and financial support from my PhD supervisor, Professor Ye Jingzhong, at COHD. During my PhD, I have had an opportunity to interact with numerous scholars who delivered public lectures in 'Critical Agrarian Studies' Lecture Series at COHD from 2011 to 2014. Those lectures gave me new insights about the agrarian studies and would often rejuvenate me to continue doing this research. I am grateful to all those people for spending time with me to discuss my work. To James Scott, whose writings, especially *Weapons of the Weak* (1985), became influential in my analysis of this work. Apart from Scott's writings, his lecture at COHD on 'Art of Not Being Governed', and post-lecture one-to-one discussion had a great influence on my work. He introduced me to some critical works on peasant politics. I am grateful to Barbara Harriss-White for spending over an hour with me, discussing my research. She introduced me to some important works on South Asia water politics.

I would like to thank the College of Humanities and Social Development at Northwest A&F University, China, for supporting my short visit to China to discuss and revise some chapters of this book.

Few people without whose inputs and proofreading, this work would not have been possible to complete. To Inam Ul Haq for always being there whenever I needed his help during the process of writing this book. Javeed ul Aziz for lending me books and giving feedback on Chapter 3 of this book. Zubair Ahmad Dar for his feedback on the initial draft of Chapter 4 of this book. Emilia Szekely for reading parts of this book. Javaid Iqbal Khan, Salma Jameel, and Tanveer Ahmad Dar for proofreading few of the chapters.

It is not possible to thank everybody who helped me in this endeavour, but there are some names I cannot miss for their friendship, encouragement, and support: Muhammad Ali Khan, Younus Rashid, Li Hua, Liu Juan, Asif Shah, Muhammad Imtiaz, Mohammad Ammad, Fernando Marcias, Tahir Usman, Muhammad Redaul Kabir, Gowhar Geelani,

Peerzada Ashiq, Khuram Parvez, Mubashir Hassan, Imran Farooq, Athar Parvez, Syeda Afshana, Dr Samir Naqash, Dr Arshad Hussain, Dr Ashraf Ganie, Jan Mohammad, and many others, whose names I might have unintentionally missed.

Thanks to the editorial team at Oxford University Press, New Delhi, for bearing with me from the last few months of this work. It was their frequent emails and messages that kept me on my toes to finish this work. Two anonymous reviewers for appreciating this work, but more importantly for providing critical feedback that helped to shape the work better. To Basharat Peer for inputs about the title of this book.

Thanks to Shuaib Masoodi for giving me the permission to use pictures of Gurez village and KHEP dam site.

This work would not have seen the light of the day had there not been unconditional love, care, guidance, and unflinching support of my family. During the process of researching and writing this work, I have gone through ups and downs. Apart from my health issues, I faced, so far, the biggest loss of my life came when my father died of cancer. After my father's death, my brothers, Nazir Masoodi and Mazoor Masoodi, looked after me and provided me with immense support and encouragement to continue my research. My nephews Suliman, Daniyal, Sayadat, Asim, little Mohammad, and my niece Khairun have given me a lot of joy. They would lift my mood when I was feeling frustrated with my work. Since I started this work I have not been able to spend much time with my mother. I cannot thank her enough for bearing with me all this time. Her prayers keep me going.

Above all, I would like to thank Almighty Allah for giving me courage, strength, and sound health to realize my dream of completing this book.

1 Capital in a Disputed Land

Land is God's vouchsafe. He asked us to work on it, it will fulfill our needs.

(*A peasant in Gurez*)

On 20 July 2000, the then Chief Minister of the disputed state of Jammu and Kashmir (henceforth Kashmir), and the Power minister of India, signed a memorandum of understanding (MoU) regarding the construction of Kishanganga Hydroelectricity Project (KHEP) alongside six other, smaller to bigger, hydroelectric projects (HEPs). The MoU was tabled before the state cabinet on 4 October 2000, and the cabinet approved the same without any detailed discussion. The construction of these HEPs was projected by the State as the solution to end the electricity scarcity of the region. This discourse was not contested, debated, or discussed in the political and civil society circles. Media reportage about the agreement also remained grossly negligible. Nevertheless, a few years after the agreement was signed, some newspaper articles hinted at the fallout of the power projects on Kashmir. These articles, followed by discussions in civil societies and political circles, coincided with the formation of new government in 2002. The new government came with a poll promise of bringing back ownership of the power projects to Kashmir—a mission for Kashmir's economic revival and energy security—as its architect and chief minister, Mufti Mohammad Sayeed, called it.

Returning of the power projects also fitted in Mufti's slogans of 'Goli Say Nahi Boli Say Baat Banay Gi' (Ballet over Bullet) and the 'healing touch'—a policy aimed at healing the wounds of conflict victims. Almost 17 months after he assumed power, Mufti wrote a letter to Prime Minister of India, Manmohan Sigh, on 7 October 2004, requesting him to transfer ownership and control of 690 megawatt (MW) Salal HEP to Jammu and Kashmir state (see Figure 1.1). While acknowledging Mufti's letter on 13 October 2004, Singh neither promised nor returned the power projects (see Figure 1.2). Mufti's rule came to an end in 2005; he returned to power again in 2014 and this time with a 'full-proof' commitment to the people that he will get the power projects back. Mufti died in January 2015, and his party also did not talk about the transfer of power projects since then—they probably realized they have neither the capacity nor the authority to get the power projects back from Government of India.

Meanwhile, exploitation of natural resources, specifically water resources, became a public discourse in Kashmir. Political parties, civil society groups, even few separatists' leaders, who were until then seeing economic sovereignty as subservient to political sovereignty, had joined this debate.

It is at this point that I started thinking about why Kashmiris feel that their resources have been grabbed by the National Hydroelectric Power Corporation (NHPC)? And, why have India and Pakistan deprived Kashmir of its water rights? I was also curious to explore why Kashmiris feel their natural resources have become a contributing factor for their 'occupation'.

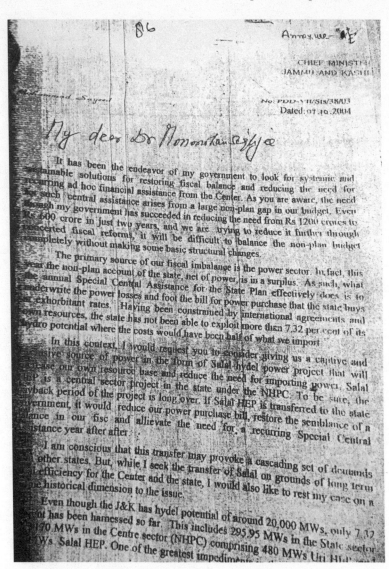

Figure 1.1   Mufti Mohammad Syeed's Letter to Manmohan Singh
Source: Report of the Cabinet Sub Committee (CSC) of the Government of Jammu and Kashmir (2011: 86–8).

H. Mohammad Sayeed

hydel sector of the State is the Indus Water Treaty signed between the Union of India and Pakistan.

Under the Indus Water Treaty, all the waters of Eastern rivers, namely Sutluj, Beas, Ravi of the Indus basin, which flow through Himachal Pradesh and Punjab, have been made available for unrestricted use of India for utilization of their water for irrigation and power. The waters of three Western rivers, namely, Chenab, Jehlum and Indus, which flow through J&K, have been made available for unrestricted use of Pakistan. Under the Indus Water Treaty there is a restriction on the total storage capacity, which can be created on the river system of Jehlum, Chenab and Indus.

Accordingly, the State Government has been forced to consider the hydroelectric schemes, as "run of the river" type only. The debilitating fall out of the arrangement is that the installed capacity of the projects in J&K is reduced. If storage was permissible it could have been utilized to store the summer discharge, which would have resulted in additional generation capacity particularly during winter months, when the demand for power is at its peak in the State. This has meant reduced power generation in the valley in the winter months due to low discharge of water. The generation goes down to 25 to 30 percent of the installed capacity during the winter months of October to March, resulting in recourse to high cost gas-based generation or a larger import of costly power from Central power stations.

The State at present can generate 1300 MUs of hydro-power which would have increased to 1750 MUs, had unrestricted storage been available. Thus the annual loss due to the restrictions on storage of our existing power house alone is Rs. 90 crores at Rs. 2.00 per unit. The loss over the life of these projects would be over Rs. 3000.00 crores. For a project of the size of Baglihar HEP (450 MW), the annual loss of the energy is estimated to be amount 1000 MUs or Rs. 200.00 crores annually and over the life of the project, it would amount to over Rs. 7,000.00 crores, for this single project alone. Considering that our hydro electric potential is about 20000 MWs, the annual energy loss would be 60,000 MUs valuing Rs. 12000 crores per year. The energy loss is colossal when compared to the total cost of individual projects like Uri-I, Rs. 3000 crores, Salal Rs. 1000 crores or even Dulhasti, Rs. 5000 crores. Even the handing over of all these projects to J&K will not compensate the state for the loss it has and will continue to sustain due to restrictions of the Indus Water T....

Figure 1.1 (Cont'd)

88

Mohammad Sayeed

The State has not been compensated for its loss so far. Instead of compensation, the State's meager share 20 MWs from the Bhakra Beas Management Board (BBMB) was also withdrawn in 1997. Likewise the construction of Uri HEP-1 by NHPC resulted in the closure of the existing State HEP at Mohra, which has not been compensated, thereby causing further loss to J&K by way of the State having to buy the same quantum of power at much higher rates from other generating stations.

It needs to be appreciated that J&K has made this great sacrifice of having forgone the control on its rivers, under the Indus Water Treaty, in the overall national interests and hence deserves full consideration of the Union Government while deciding on this important issue of compensation.

To recapitulate, in order to find a long term solution to these problems faced by the State, I would seek your judicious and far sighted intervention to :

a) Transfer 690 MW Salal HEP, which has paid back more than debt and equity investment of NHPC, to the State Government;

b) To make J&K a fully participatory State for sharing of power generated of the Eastern rivers allotted to India in lieu of the waters of Western rivers flowing through J&K which had been made available for use of Pakistan to the disadvantage of our State.

Yours Sincerely

(Mufti Mohammad Sayeed)

Dr. Manmohan Singh,
Hon'ble Prime Minister
South Block,
New Delhi, 110001

o/c

Copy forwarder to the :-

1. Economic Advisor to Hon'ble CM.
2. Principal Secretary to Govt. Planning & Dev. Deptt
3. Special Asstt. to Hon'ble MOP.
4. Pvt. Secretary to Hon'ble MOS(Power)

Figure 1.1 *(Cont'd)*

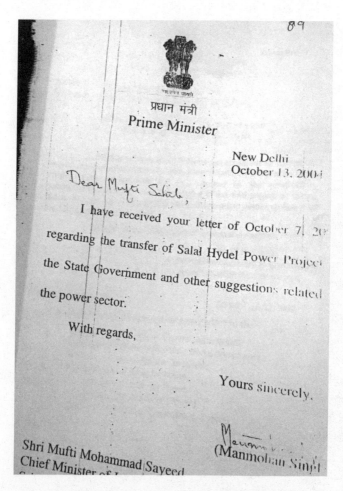

Figure 1.2   Manmohan Singh's Letter of Acknowledgement
Source: Report of the Cabinet Sub Committee (CSC) of the Government of Jammu and Kashmir Government (2011: 89).

To address this curiosity, I decided to visit Gurez, where NHPC is building a dam for 330 MW KHEP. It was June 2011 when I planned to take this journey to understand how capital works in one of the most militarized and landlocked areas of Kashmir. Even though I was born in Kupwara, arguably the most militarized districts in Kashmir, yet Gurez located on India–Pakistan border, was something unimaginable for me to visit, due to its heavy military presence. Thus it took me more time to prepare and plan for this approximately 150 kilometre journey from Srinagar to Gurez, than I have ever planned for any foreign trip. I contacted my friends in Kashmir and asked them if they had been to Gurez. A journalist friend replied that he has been there once. It was a relief to me. I explained to him that I want to visit Gurez for this study and to know more about the place, the issues of security, the food I can eat, and the places I can stay—in short the issues that are not being covered in mainstream media. In this 20 minutes phone call, he answered all my queries. Apart from other dos and don'ts, he advised me to travel early morning so that I can get a travel permit—a permission card issued by district police chief at district headquarter Bandipora. While I had a curiosity turned commitment to travel to this place, I also had apprehensions about my security. My family had the same apprehensions. So I asked some friends to accompany me. Few of them agreed to join me to visit this beautiful place. We all boarded a car and reached Bandipora district headquarters. Upon arriving in Bandipora town, we inquired about the district police chief's—Superintendent of Police (SP)—office to apply for a travel permit. Upon arriving at the SP's office, located on the banks of the river, we were informed that the SP was in Srinagar for a meeting. One police official in the SP's office advised us to wait for a few hours until he returns to Bandipora. It was already 12:30 p.m. Waiting for two more hours for the SP, followed by 30 minutes procedure to prepare the travel documents, would mean that we could only proceed for Gurez at 3 p.m. We pleaded with the police official to expedite the procedure of permit application, as we have been advised by local people to leave for Gurez before 2 p.m. The policemen showed helplessness. 'I am not authorized to issue this permit', he told me. But a few minutes later he came out of his room and asked us to follow him to meet his boss, the additional SP of the district, who he believed had an authority to issue this permit. While entering the office of the additional SP, I saw this tall police official sitting in his office. Before I could introduce ourselves, the official smiled and said, 'Did you recognize me?' I replied, 'No, I didn't'. As soon as he revealed his name, I could recognize this official as one of my acquaintances who was posted in Srinagar a few years ago. He inquired why we were going to Gurez. After inquiring about the purpose of our visit, he asked us to submit an application with an identity proof and two passport size photographs. After completing the procedure, he asked his subordinates to get the permit cards readied quickly. It took us 20 minutes to get the permit cards. He further asked his subordinates to explain to us the whole procedure about when, where, and how we have to show and produce this card during our journey to Gurez. We left the SP's office at 1:30 p.m. and proceeded towards Gurez.

The valley, with lush green meadows, pine forests and a trout-filled Kishanganga river which comes through rich meadows, falls on the road that connects Kashmir to Central Asia and China through Silk Route from Gilgit Baltistan in Pakistan. Located at the Indo-Pakistan border, travelling to this approximately 150 kilometre journey from Srinagar to Gurez was a herculean task; as it takes a seven hours zigzag drive, transcending 1,200 metre Razdan top to reach Gurez town, but not before you show your permit card at various army check posts—the last one being two kilometres before Daver—centre of Gurez. The permit card has to be shown at each check post while returning back from Gurez. Upon arriving, the first thing I realized was that Gurezees were living in, what social theorist Michael Foucault (1980) identified as, a 'continuous and permanent system of surveillance' of Indian Army and intelligence agencies.

We reached Gurez at around 8 p.m. and stayed in the Tourist Guest House at Daver, which is five kilometres from Badwan and seven kilometres from Khopri—KHEP dam site. Next morning I visited Badwan and Khopri for initial interaction about the KHEP and other power projects in Kashmir. For the next few days, I had threadbare discussions with the village heads, the village watchman, and other people from the villages, besides officials from the Hindustan Construction Company (HCC), which earned a contract from the NHPC to build KHEP. Peasants initially took me as a journalist, as some journalists had visited the villages to report about the HEP, but no research scholar till date had gone to study KHEP. Nevertheless, during my subsequent discussions with the peasants of Badwan and Khopri, I found out that their concerns were much different than the concerns

Table 1.1 Stakeholder Positions and Interests

Geopolitics	Hydropower Politics	Water Politics Indus Water Treaty	Capital	Peasants
India	Kashmir Politics, The State of J&K	Kashmir	NHPC	NHPC/ HCC
Pakistan	India	India	State of Kashmir	State of Kashmir Kashmir Politics
Kashmir Politics (KP)	Pakistan	Pakistan	Foreign Capital	Absentee Landlords

Source: Author.

of larger Kashmiri community. For them it was immediate fallouts of KHEP on their land, houses, and livelihoods than the larger case of exploitation of resources by the corporation advocated by the Kashmiri political parties and civil society.

Gurez posed more questions than it answered for me. Questions like, where does the peasant discourse fit into the India–Pakistan water politics or Kashmir-India politics, for example. Thus, I attempted to locate concerns of the peasantry in India–Pakistan water politics and Indian hydropower politics. For understanding stakeholder positions and interests see Table 1.1.

Indus Water Treaty and Hydropower Politics

Just a few months after India and Pakistan came into existence, they realized that modalities of Partition were still incomplete, when on 1 April 1948 India stopped water from Satluj river from flowing into West Pakistan, which irrigates 8 per cent of the cultivable area of Pakistan (Dar 2011–2). This made it clear that a water-sharing agreement between the countries was crucial for the survival of these two countries. Thus, with the intervention of the World Bank, the Indus Water Treaty (IWT) was signed between India and Pakistan in 1960. Article III of the treaty, for which the World Bank is also a signatory, allows Pakistan unrestrictive use of waters from the western rivers of Indus-basin—Indus, Jhelum, and Chenab—which flow through the disputed territory of Kashmir and enter West Punjab in Pakistan. India, being in control of part of Kashmir, has been given rights to use the water for domestic use, non-consumptive use, agriculture use, and hydroelectricity use, on the basis of 'run-of-the-river' plant that 'develops electricity without live storage as an integral part of the plant, except for poundage and surcharge storage' (IWT Annexure D, part 3). On the other hand, Article II of IWT gives India unrestrictive use of the water of eastern rivers—Satluj, Ravi, and Beas. However, Pakistan can use waters of these rivers for irrigation and other agricultural purposes.

With the signing of the IWT, Pakistan might have thought that the problem of water-sharing was over. However, just two decades later it proved wrong, at least from the Pakistani perspective, when India planned to develop Salal HEP. In accordance with the IWT rules, India informed Pakistan about the project plan. Pakistan, after checking the details, objected to the project design. Its objections were based on the possibility that the storage and diversion of waters would create irrigation problems in Pakistan. Moreover, it feared that India could use the dam water to flood major parts of Pakistan in times of war (Dar 2011–12; Wirsing and Jasparro 2006). Ultimately, external expert observations suggested modifications in the dam and project plan, which addressed Pakistani worries, and therefore it accepted India's new plan. Soon after Salal HEP, the NHPC started developing a new project, Dulhasti HEP. Here again Pakistan raised objections about the project, however, things were amicably resolved. Nonetheless, the Pakistani people saw these projects as part of India's mission to destroy Pakistan.

Amidst rising dissatisfaction among the Pakistani people, in 1992, three years after Kashmir's armed uprising against Indian rule began, Pakistani militants operating in Kashmir abducted a French engineer who was working on the project. In a similar fashion, two engineers from the Uri HEP were abducted, who were later released after 72 days of captivity. The abduction of these engineers caused a delay in the project.

A decade after India planned to build the next HEP, the Kishanganga Project, Pakistan expressed strong reservations against the HEP construction. Pakistan's objection was on the basis that, (*a*) the inter-tributary diversion is barred by the treaty, and the water drawn from a given tributary must be returned to the same river, (*b*) the existing Pakistani usage must be protected as India's Kishanganga Project will deprive it of 27 per cent of the river's natural flow, thereby inflicting damage to its existing 133,000 hectares of irrigation in the Neelum Valley and a 900 MW under construction Neelum–Jhelum hydro project at Muzaffarabad, and (*c*) the HEP design features are not in conformity with IWT.

With Pakistan exerting pressure on India to modify the project design, according to the IWT agreement, India changed the model of the dam from 73 metres high to 37 metres high (Dar 2011–2). However, Pakistan still did not agree with the plan and informed India that it would take the case to the International Court of Arbitration (ICA) if India did not stop work on the project. While India stressed that the dam construction was in accordance with the IWT norms, Pakistan took the case to the ICA in Hague in May 2010. As the two countries did not reach an agreement on the nomination of three neutral judges for the hearing of the case, they instead invoked the provision of IWT under which UN Secretary General, Ban Ki-moon, nominated Stephen M. Schwebel, a former president of ICA, as the head of the seven-member arbitration bench. In October 2011, Schwebel lead seven-member bench, which included two nominated members from each country, asked India to stop work on Kishanganga until the court gave a final order. But, India never stopped work on the ground. In February 2013, the court gave its interim judgement regarding diversion of waters, and concluded that the diversion of water did not go against the IWT norms, because the water was being released back to its natural route and the construction of the dam had not violated IWT norms. This judgement was celebrated in India as India's success of following IWT norms. In Pakistan the judgement was seen with scepticism and criticism on the government for not pleading the case of the country properly in ICA. Yet the government of Pakistan invoked the hope in the final judgemental in favour of it, the hearing of which was scheduled in December 2013 (Tiwari 2013; Wasim 2013). The ICA, in its final judgement in December 2013, upheld its initial decision that India was within IWT rights to divert the waters and build the Kishanganga HEP, as the diversion did not go against IWT, and India had officially commenced work on the HEP much before Pakistan's Neelum–Jhelum HEP. However, at the same time, the court issued an order that India needs to release 50 per cent flow of water downstream in the Neelum valley. While Pakistan's ruling party marketed it as Pakistan's success (*Daily Times* 2013), the civil society actors and other political activists blamed Pakistani Government for misrepresenting the case at ICA, by not providing enough data about the losses occurring to agricultural sector due to the diversion of the water (Abbasi 2013). The court's decision left Pakistan with no option except to accept the ICA judgement. As India is on a move to build many more HEPs, Pakistan's political parties have made it a political agenda to fight against these HEPs, with some even going to the extent that these projects can cause nuclear war in the region. A Pakistani academician, Ansoor Ahmad, described the construction of HEPs as India's strategy to control waters that can lead to war.

> Look at the Neelum Valley, these projects have led a huge impact on our agriculture. We want to develop our own electricity, but India controls and diverts the waters. But if India keeps doing the same thing, it will not just remain debate on the diplomatic or political level; rather it can cause a war between the two nations ... and let me stress on one point that this war will be a nuclear war.

While there is a difference of opinion between the two countries on water sharing, the IWT has been globally seen as one of the finest models of intra-state water agreement, which offers a win-win solution for both countries.

But Kashmir's scholars, political leaders, civil society groups, and many other sections of the society have observed it as, an injustice done to the people of the region by not giving them water rights despite the water flowing through its territory. The following two statements of an

Table 1.2   Total Storage of Water Permitted to J&K under IWT in Million Acres Feet (MAF)

River System	General Storage Capacity (A)	Power Storage Capacity (B)	Flood Storage Capacity (C)	Total Storage Capacity (A+B+C)
Indus	0.25	0.15	Nil	0.40 MAF
The Jehlum	0.50	0.25	0.75	1.50 MAF
The Chenab including Chenab main and tributaries	0.50	1.20	Nil	1.70

Source: Majeed (2015: 101).

academic and a civil society activist, and the data presented in Table 1.2 reflect that concern.

> More near to our times, while India and Pakistan had to share the resources and assets of undivided India as per the conditions and principles of partition, they appropriated again what actually never belonged to them, in lieu of east Punjab rivers on which both the, now divided, Punjab had equal rights as being their common inheritance. Whereas Punjab(s) emerged as a principle beneficiary, proverbial poor Kashmiri was the principle loser. The then (1960) Prime Minister of Kashmir was made to congratulate the two beneficiaries of the Indus water treaty for what was destined to become a major water related developmental hazard to Kashmir. (Majeed 2015: 99)

> Because of the IWT we have immensely suffered on account of producing hydro-electricity. Under this treaty we cannot build dams, beyond specified height prescribed in this treaty. Moreover, all the power projects have to be made on the run-of-the-river. We cannot store water, so the optimization of the electricity project varies ... because from time to time water levels vary ... in winters it decreases but in summers it increases. However, during summers we cannot harness the potential of electricity; this treaty is at worst to the interest of Kashmir. (Author interview with a trade union leader and head of a civil society group, June 2012)

Interestingly, the importance of IWT and its fulfilment of the interests of both the countries can be gauged from the fact that IWT has withstood three wars between the two countries. In Kashmir, the visible posturing of India and Pakistan is now seen differently, as both countries not only have a strategic geo-political interest but also underlying economic interests which are concerned with who owns/controls the waters and how. A political scientist based in Kashmir explained:

> In the 1950s, when Kashmir was being discussed hotly between India and Pakistan, very few of us realized at that stage that the Kashmir issue was not purely pertaining to secularism and nationalism or religious nationalism or secular nationalism, as was being projected to us. However, in the early 1960s it became clear that how significant the state is as far as the flow of water to Pakistan is concerned. (Author interview with a political scientist based in Srinagar, July 2012)

While IWT did not serve the interests of the Kashmiri people has been established by the literature (CSC 2011; Dar 2011–12; Majeed 2015) at the same time, violation of agreements and land and water grabs by India's Public Sector Undertakings (PSU), such as, National Hydroelectric Power Corporation (NHPC) is seen as the extension of resource exploitation in Kashmir. (Apart from this chapter, we shall also discuss the resource exploitation and violation of agreements in Chapters 5, 6, and 7.)

National Hydroelectric Power Corporation was established by the Government of India in 1976 as an independent electricity development corporation with an investment of 2,000 crore rupees. In 1978, Salal HEP, for which a memorandum of understanding (MoU) was signed between the Government of India and the Government of Jammu and Kashmir, was entrusted to NHPC for execution. The first phase of the project was commissioned in 1978 and the second phase in 1996. Over the years, electricity from these projects has been supplied to expanding Indian cities to cater to the electricity needs of the growing middle class of India and the new industrial sector. Projects of this scale have transformed NHPC from a small enterprise to one among the top 10 PSUs in India.

No doubt, in mainland India, NHPC is considered a corporation that has been generating electricity for energy hungry corporation in India and building 'sacred' infrastructure in Kashmir that strengthens India's presence in Kashmir. However, in Kashmir valley, right from Salal HEP-I to KHEP, NHPC has been accused of exploiting the resources of Kashmir, violating contracts, cheating, and bribing bureaucrats to get an unfair advantage (see further details about NHPC exploitation in the proceeding sections of this chapter and in Chapters 5, 6, and 7).

As these HEPs are being constructed, there is a growing debate among the political, social, and academic circles, about the fallout of these projects on the Kashmir's political economy and its natural resources. Voices in the Kashmir valley from across the political spectrum are now becoming louder against this exploitation. Over the years, state ministers, politicians and other civil society actors have been very vocal against this exploitation, with many politicians even going to the extent of referring to NHPC as 'East India Company' (EIC).[1] This is perhaps the only issue where the mainstream and separatist leaders of Kashmir are fighting for a common cause—against the economic injustices done to the region. A former state minister for irrigation and a member of Indian National Congress Party described NHPC as a cheater, which has no legal base in Kashmir:

> NHPC has no legal base here. The ownership of any project or of land has not been given to them. We have never even leased land to them. They are occupiers. What has happened, when NHPC floated Initial Public Offering (IPO), they showed their flagship projects and programs. And the most terrible thing they did even with their shareholders is that they deceived them by saying that they own the Salal and Uri HEPs. What I want to tell their shareholders is NHPC is a cheater, who fraudulently stole the agreement documents from the state government offices,

---

[1] East India Company entered India as a trading company but later expanded it base, thus leading to the colonization of India, with support of the British government. Economic historians have criticized the company for exploiting Indian natural resources (see detailed account on EIC exploitation in Chapter 3).

including the governor's office and it is illegally occupying the land here, and extracting resources of Kashmir like British East India Company did before 1947 in the Indian subcontinent. (Author interview with Minister of Irrigation and Water Works, Kashmir Government, June 2012)

As Henry Veltmeyer (2013) argues, 'capitalism has been always based on the extraction of natural resources and exploitation of labour and imperialism is exploitation of these resources for the state.' Thus NHPC, as I argue—see Chapter 5, 6, and 7—which grabs lands, exploits labour for its profit and for national development, represents both capitalism and imperialism in Kashmir.

While as the NHPC is bracketed as imperialistic for exploitation of resources, specifically water in Kashmir; ironically, resources extractions by Jammu and Kashmir State Power Development Corporation (JKPDC)—state's own agency for power generation is described in Kashmir as 'cost-worth-taking' for the national (Kashmiri) development. In fact, HEPs such as Bagliyar run or commissioned by JKPDC are projected and showcased as 'state-of-the-art' for its 'marvellous' engineering work and an 'epitome of capability' of the local human resource to bring home a point that Kashmiris have potential to develop and run HEPs affectively. This is aimed to deconstruct the mainstream Indian perspective that Kashmiris are not capable of running HEPs, therefore HEPs cannot be transferred to them—a demand from Kashmir.

While IWT, hydro politics in India and Pakistan, and role of NHPC in exploiting water and land resources of Kashmir catches frequent newspaper headlines and have become subject of many academic studies in Kashmir and South Asia; however, dispossession and displacement of thousands of peasants in Kashmir due to land-grabs by the same corporation has not generated much debate in media or in academic studies. Even civil society and human rights groups have not raised the issue of displacement and dispossessions of peasantry due to these land-grabs. While it may be stated that the 'depeasantization', dispossession, and displacement caused by these HEPs in Kashmir can be clubbed with the regime of dispossession and displacement of Nehruvian development model,[2] however, what is argued here is the depeasantization, dispossession, and displacement in Kashmir are purely state-induced and state directed, whereby the existence of 'state of exception', through the presence of Armed Forces Special Power Act (AFSPA) together with use of 'extra-economic coercion' makes the land acquisition possible without any strong resentment against it (Agamben 2005).

Within this background, I tried to locate and place land-grabs and peasant politics in the larger land-grabbing debate, wherein large-scale land acquisitions, resource extractions, and water control by the national and multinational corporations, are described as 'global land-grab'. Thus land-grabs have become a 'catch-all' phrase for a sizable section of academia, human rights activists, non-governmental organizations (NGOs), and some mainstream development practitioners and scholars. 'Land-grab' is generally defined as the large-scale lease or purchase of land by domestic or international corporations for agricultural production or for industry. Recently, land acquisition by the state, where there is no clear public purpose defined, is also bracketed as a 'land-grab'. This does not mean that the state is not involved in the corporate-led land-grabs (see Chapters 2, 4, and 5). The state plays a pivotal role in all the land deals. While land-grabs loosely refer to the large-scale land expropriations by foreign companies from Global South in the Global North, however land-grabs have been taking place from north to south, south to south, south to north, and inside the countries by the national corporations (Borras and Franco 2012). Graham et al. (2010: 17) defines 'land-grabbing' as, 'taking possession of and/or controlling a scale of land which is disproportionate in size in comparison to average land holdings in the region'. Others describe 'land-grabbing' actually as 'control-grabbing' that infers power to control land and allied resources (Borras et al. 2012).

As Wolf (1969) points out that no definition is absolute and they are just tools to support in analysis, this book, therefore, taking a leaf from

---

[2] Development of steel mills, scientific forestry, dams, and so on (see Micheal Levien [2011] for further discussion on the state of development in Nehru era).

Graham et al.'s (2010) and Borras et al.'s (2012) studies and describes land-grabbing as forcible acquisition or control of land and waters, changes in water use and water tenure relations, and diversion of the water from its natural flow, by the national or transnational corporations, with or without the hard or soft support of the State, for the 'public purpose' and 'national' or 'sub-national security' purpose. Here the focus is quite akin with Sara Safransky and Wendy Wolford's (2011) arguments, where they stress more on understanding 'extraction' and 'alienation' caused by the land-grabs than the capital invested in it or its intended market. Besides Safransky and Wolford framing, I stress on forced commoditization, dispossession, displacement, impacts on culture, tradition, jobs, and so on, which I argue in Chapter 6, leads to resistance and is of utmost importance in understanding land politics and rural development.

To see through the prism of mainstream economic view, which treats industrialization and urbanization as synonymous with development; industrialization-led urbanization requires land for its expansion or operation. For the expansion of industrialization, the land is provided or facilitated by the state to fit its 'rural development' process. In this process of land acquisition or 'land-grabs' people are being dispossessed, displaced, and their livelihoods are being snatched to transfer the land to corporations for the so called development (Bhaduri 2007; Sing 1997). In general terms, the present rural development model in developing and least developed countries, is the expansion of industrial capitalism led by the development model which has been utterly dominated and defined by USA, Europe, and the new economic giants of East Asia.

As the population of the world is touching 7 billion and is estimated to reach up to 9.2 billion by 2050, with 75 per cent of it still dependent on farming (Aljazeera 2011), coupled with rapid urbanization, there will be more pressure on land. This pressure to produce more food for increasing population, through industrial farming, and to support large scale industrial corporate-led development has led to large scale land-grabbing in developing and least developed countries under the garb of 'food security', and need for rapid industrialization. At the same time, shrinking of the arable land, puts more pressure on the existing landmass. International Fund for Agriculture Development (2008: 17) mentions, that 5–10 hectares of agriculture land is lost, annually globally, due to soil degradation. The number might be a bit exaggerated, but the worrying factor is arable land is shrinking, midst the increasing demand of land for industrialization; which will create a further challenge of local food security. In Asia, 95 per cent of cropland has been already put under utilization, while at the same time, the process of industrial-led urbanization is at its peak. The challenge is how much pressure corporate investment will put on the cropland. So, even if the small amount of cropland is taken for corporate development, it will certainly have an impact on the local food sovereignty. It is not only the impact on the crop land, but on government-owned land, forest land, private non-farming and other forms of land which is given away for the corporate investment, and which has a potential to create corporate colonization in these countries.

Many researchers have discussed the issues of land-grab from left, right, and centre perspectives. Mainstream economic-development scholars and institutions argue to push for corporate investment in land, in a view, what they call is a prime chance to get corporate investment in rural areas. Thus it provides, what they call, opportunities for development in the rural areas. On the other side of the fence are scholars and human rights activists who with equal force, argue that these land deals are often shady, violate local cultural and traditional norms, disposes people from their land and property, create dependence on market, reshape livelihood structures, and thus create what is known as forced commoditization, and above all does not provide the benefits—employment and poverty alleviation—which these land deals promise to do (Li 2011; Mishra 2011).

Since India opened its economy in 1991, it embraced, though partially, the neo-liberal development model. This development model encouraged industrialization, which obviously requires land. The land is a state subject as per the Constitution of India, therefore, the state can acquire land for 'public purpose'. Under this garb of 'public purpose', Indian federal states projected corporate investment as necessary for rural development. Thus, began the rat race as to which state brings more capital investment. And, for getting the corporate investment, they acquire land (Bhaduri 2007). Besides the grabbing of private-owned land, huge chunks of government-owned land under the possession and cultivation of local people is given to outsiders not only in India but in other developing countries as well (Cuffaro and Hallam 2011). This process of land acquisition in a place like India, where above 60 per cent of the population is still dependent on land, brings us to the question about the survival of those people. We shall discuss global land-grabbing in Chapter 2 of this book.

Nevertheless, unlike land-grabs in mainland India, which are neo-liberal in orientation, land-grabs in the disputed Kashmir region are state directed for market forces. Given its mountainous terrain and ongoing conflict in the region, India's opening up of the economy in the 1990s and the subsequent rush for land by market forces, was not however seen here. Kashmir could not become a space for neo-liberal forces to grab land due to the emergence of insurgency, which coincided with opening of India for economic liberalization, and did not become a source of attraction for investors on farmland either after the 2008 food crisis, as the quantum of arable land is very small in the region. It is pertinent to mention here that land-grabbers focus on the countries and places where agriculture pro-duction could be enhanced with the application of technology (Rulli et al. 2013: 4), and in the case of Kashmir, it is nearly impossible due to small land holdings. Nevertheless, Kashmir could not keep itself aloof from land-grabbing. Kashmiri lands became the focus of grabbers for the avail-ability of water resources for electricity generation. No doubt situating land-grabs in Kashmir within the global land-grabbing is critically impor-tant, as it has been done here. However, land-grabbing in Kashmir has to be understood in the context of disputed nature of the region and in the ongoing political and armed struggle. Land-grabbing in Kashmir cannot be also analysed within the framework of 'resource-curse', which has been a by-product of modernization and wherein armed and political resistance has been launched against these resource extractions. For example, in Chittagong in Bangladesh; Xinjiang and Tibet in China; Baluchistan, Gilgit, parts in Khyber Pakhtunkhwa, and Pakistan-administered-Kashmir in Pakistan; Cambodia; north-east states of India; Myanmar;

and others. The extreme use of force by the state to control resources—land, water, and minerals, among others—has led to wars and insurgencies in and around 200 regions at the present time. As Scott (2010) argues, 'historically every state has extracted from the country side and feed the urban areas'. The regions which were earlier ignored, neglected, or did not even find mention in the footnotes of populist literature, newspapers, and others, before the advent of industrialization, became very important in terms of their resources in the twentieth century. Land-grabs in some of these conflict-hit regions have different patterns than the land-grabbing happening in the so called peaceful regions and countries. Nevertheless, most of these movements against resource extraction are fought within the ambit of the constitution of the countries. Land-grabs in disputed territories such as in Palestine and Kashmir however, stand out from the rest of the conflict regions. This work thus becomes the first account of land-grabbing in a conflict zone.

This work should not be read for that reason only. Land-grabs in Kashmir also go beyond the macro picture of the land-grabbing debate and present a case study of two villages in the extreme north of Kashmir. While piles of research has been done on global land-grabs, there exists an inconsistency and ineffectual data has been produced in these large studies, which makes land-grab studies weak to defend (Edelman 2013; Oya 2013). Gitelman and Jackson (cited in Edelman 2013: 6) question and beautifully deconstruct the validity of large database:

They pile up. They are collected in assortments of individual, homologous data entries and are accumulated into larger or smaller data sets. This aggregative quality of data helps to lend them their potential power, their rhetorical weight. (More is better, isn't it?) Indeed, data are so aggregative that English usage increasingly makes many into one. The word data has become what is called a mass noun, so it can take a singular verb. Sentences that include the phrase 'data is ...' are now roughly four times as common ... as those including 'data are ...' despite countless grammarians out there who will insist that data is a plural.

Therefore, realizing that large land deals data is problematic, and ethnographic micro-focused study is labour intensive and less useful in making claims about large scale land-grabbing trends, nonetheless, they have potential to uncover ground realities of land politics without making false or ineffectual claims (Edelman 2013). Within this dynamics, Kashmir was chosen as a case study. However, choosing Kashmir as a study area has many other important reasons as well. For example, since the partition of Indian subcontinent, numerous distinguished scholars have studied the political history and specific struggles of Kashmir (Behera 2006; Bhan 2014; Bose 2003; Lamb 1991; Peer and Ye 2015; Schofield 2003). However, till now, little effort has been made to understand how the HEPs construction dispossessed and displaced the peasants. Furthermore, a huge amount of literature, as you would see in Chapter 2, about land, development, water, and agriculture was produced by the scholars on India, however, Kashmir was largely neglected in this scholarship. This was, as Aziz (2010: iv) puts it:

The fact that although there had been an overwhelming presence of state economies in the overall level of economic activity of the country, however, the spotlight had traditionally been on national macro-economic situation and there was a lack of adequate appreciation of the potential of sub- national economies.

This trend however changed with the emergence of postmodern studies in the 1980s when regional/micro studies were seen as being of utmost important, and development studies started to put their focus on regional studies (Brass 1999). With rising interest in regional studies, which coincided with the opening of Indian economy—from a so called rigid to market friendly one—thus brought the focus of scholars to study sub-national economies, agrarian structures, and local histories. However, this was the phase when Kashmir's insurgency began, and thus scholars focused more on Kashmir's political struggles than the agrarian structure, peasant rights, and water politics. While the 'movement' for independence is ongoing, so is the scholarship on Kashmir confined to understanding the political struggle. The peasantry on the other hand, which has been displaced and dispossessed over the years, due to HEPs, gets no mention even in the footnotes of history. Therefore understanding land-grabs in Kashmir, and politics and power around these grabs, is not about understanding just the land-grabs of a state in India, but Kashmir is a case *sui generis* in Indian Constitution, where laws passed by Indian Parliament cannot be directly applied to the state, as it has its own constitution and land laws, unlike other states of India.

The case of Kashmiri land-grabs is also chosen for the fact that these waters and HEPs have become a bone of contention between the two South Asian nuclear armed nations—India and Pakistan. The construction of dams and HEPs in Kashmir has been described by many people as a possible reason for future war between the two nations. Thus, this makes the study of land-grabs not only locally important, but understanding the narratives of different actors, as explained in this study, very important for the larger geo-politics of the South Asian region. Furthermore, land-grabs in Kashmir also provide an account of understanding and explaining such grabs, processes, and impacts in other disputed and conflict zones, which existing literature fails to do.

This book majorly focuses on the narratives and resistance surrounding these land-grabs. The very fact of resisting or not resisting the land-grab is an important area to look at while understanding the industrial agro-development project or the expansion of rural development project, for which these land-grabs take place. It makes an attempt to explain why some people resist land-grab while others do not? What are the pushes and pulls that force/motivate peasants to or not to resist. And, secondly, the other area which has not been addressed or focused in the literature yet, is: Why do people resist these land deals, if they are given 'enough' compensation? Are these people anti-development, as they are being branded? Or they are not aware of, as being often told by mainstream development experts and their affiliates in governments, the 'development fortunes' brought by this investment? Whatever be the case, understanding reasons and ways and mechanisms of resistance to these 'global land-grabs' is a very important element to look at in the larger land-grab debate, and in particular, the capitalist led rural development and people's response to these land deals.

I entered the field asking 'why' and 'why not' questions. Here I have tried to explain how narratives shape resistance in the politically volatile situation, such as in Kashmir. And, how state allows resistance at a certain place while it facilitates land-grabs at the same breath.

Therefore, this research is unique in two senses: (*a*) it asks the questions: how state, elites, and absentee landlords create narratives to justify land-grabs and how subalterns/peasants respond to this notion through their narratives? It does so, by not relying only on one perspective but multiple perspectives as mentioned above. And (*b*) it focuses on the region which offers a variety of forms of resistance to land-grabs, however, not interpreted, explained, or theorized academically. I believe this research breaks the path of understanding the question of land politics, power, and politics around the land- and water-grabbing, the impacts of these land and water grabs, and how these impacts shape resistance and narratives of the actors involved in this particular setting, which may be relevant in other similar settings.

In this book I employ ethnographic, political sociology, historical, and political economy methods to understand the power politics of land-grabbing. Ethnographic studies or smaller level studies, as they are known now, try to understand the phenomenon in social, cultural, and historical contexts (Lewis 1985: 380). This method can be done through long informal interviews, direct observation, group discussions, class room participation, and participation in rituals, celebrations, and mourning, and so on. Ethnographic method is an inductive method which tries to build the theory on the basis of the data on the ground. It is, as Neumann (2003: 146) explained, 'theory is built from data or grounded in that data. Moreover, conceptualization and operationalization of data occur simultaneously with data collection and preliminary data analysis'. The benefit of doing informal interviews is to get the clear understanding of the phenomena you are observing, and more importantly to understand the complex social relations without giving a sense of policing to the respondents. Following this tradition, here the attempt was made to understand the phenomena by applying interpretive social science research method, which as pointed out by Neumann (2003: 75) helps to understand 'the personal reasons or motives that shape the internal feelings and guide decisions to act in a particular way'. Interpretive social science believes that social life or reality is socially constructed and thus it stresses on the point that multiple realities can occur as people start communicating/interacting with each other and their environment.

Within these dynamics, this work goes deep into understanding narratives of different actors, the meaning behinds the narratives, the meaning of land, power, water, home, jobs, and so on. This is because narratives, life histories, and stories are powerful tools to understand a social phenomenon. Narratives in the village or rural context are more useful, as most of the people are illiterate and written records are often absent. Thus oral narratives provide grassroots information about the village happenings, history, culture, changes, as well as people's actions and reactions to the changes. Therefore this book is about storytelling. It talks about the meanings, relations, and connections of the peasants with the land, water, and natural habitat. It is about the actions and reactions to the political and elite power from the below. It also explains the intricacies of owning and losing the material and non-material resources. While acknowledging that the narratives have their short comings, such as, 'narratives are always immersed in history and never innocent' (Escobar 1995: 20). Nevertheless, life stories reflect the culture where they are created or told (McAdams 2006). Even though, people's memory fades with the passage of time, and they may not accurately remember the events which have happened in the past, yet it is the narrative which defines and explains the embedded power relation of the development and underdevelopment, the power to decide and control and the power to own and disown.

My study has thus taken a path in which I had no questionnaire in hand and no questions in mind. I went to the field holding a stick like a blind person who is directed by a stick and not directs the sticks.

In the process of reading this book you will find a mix of academic analysis and journalistic and social activist account. I believe it is all of that.

Thus, in Chapter 2 of this book, I place Kashmir land-grabs in the global land-grabs debate. Here I provide a detailed and critical account of the dominant assumptions about the current wave of land-grabbing—its features, impacts, and narratives. This chapter discusses the property rights, actors, and power relations surrounding land-grabs and development led dispossession and displacement. Moreover, the chapter interrogates literature on resistance to the land and water grabs. This chapter further discusses land and water-grabs literature in India.

To understand land-grabs in Kashmir through a historical lens, Chapter 3 traces the roots of colonization in India and explains how peasants/political and social movements arose against the British East India Company rule. This is done to understand the land-grabs in Kashmir through the historical lens. The chapter puts light on how the British enacted and controlled the land and resources, and how these laws have had an effect on India even after Independence. The chapter further gives the account of how India used nationalistic development policy, after it got independence. And during the process of this development policy of constructing dams, steel plants, and so on, how they were projected as part of nationalistic agenda and the land was neglected over 'Temples of India'[3]—dams and steel plants. Furthermore, the chapter describes how land acquired the important position in the policy and political debate in India after the reforms of 1991, and majorly after the formation of the special economic zones (SEZs). After explaining the history of land relations in India and the emergence of land-grabbing era, the chapter also explains Kashmir's relation with India, as a state *sui generis*, how the power projects, the political relation between the region and the country shaped since it made contested 'accession' with India.

Chapter 4 provides a historical account of land rights and land tenure changes in Kashmir. Further it also looks into the land reforms in

---

[3] Nehru called dams and steel plants as 'Temples of India'. To him dams and steel plants were to bring economic revolution in India. They were projected as 'sacred', though in political and economic sense. Thus any resistance against them was not tolerated.

Kashmir, and how these reforms look like and how they took place. An explanation of as to how the peasant land rights were restored again due to land reforms is also a part of this chapter. I also discuss in the chapter that while the land reforms provided land to the tiller, however, it did not stop them from getting dispossessed and displaced during the current wave of land-grabbing. Here I also explain the historical background of Badwan and Khopri, besides presenting the geographical, administrative, and brief socio-economic sketch of the two villages. NHPC functioning in the state, the process of land acquisition, and the arrival of external capital in Gurez is also explained. The chapter gives a detailed account of arbitrary control of land by the state.

In Chapter 5 an attempt is made to critically examine the class dynamics of land control. In that chapter I go on to explain the elite influence, which is quite prominent in the decision-making process. It explains the process and means through which absentee landlords take decisions on behalf of subsistent peasantry. Yet on the other layer, here I explain the inter-dependence of the poor on the elites and vice versa. At the same time the chapter shows the peasant narratives about subordination, subalternity, and powerlessness, and at the end, control on lands. The chapter further looks into the process of having and losing. It mainly explains the peasant's interpretations of losses caused by dispossession and displacements. It also brings together the viewpoints of the state, corporates, and political parties on the concept of the micro picture of who gets what and how.

Furthermore, the chapter explains how HEP construction caused the destruction of ecology and how peasants lost their rights on common property resources. The HEP construction affects the water bodies, forests, pasture areas, which are home to many species of birds, fisheries, and animals, and to the people who have a dependence on these community property resources. Moreover, the chapter explains how land-grabbing leads to a phenomenon where land is needed while labour is not. It stresses on how peasants are exploited, in the name of employment, by politicians and corporations.

In Chapter 6, I discuss the historical account of peasant's resistance to the land-grabs in Kashmir. Here, I describe how people fought the lonely battle to stop land-grabbing, whereby neither media nor the local administration or civil society supported them. With the resistance against land-grabbing not yielding positive results, I explain how peasants made the transition from resistance against land-grabs to resistance for compensation. Besides peasants' resistance, the chapter also describes the external dimensions of resistance to KHEP which comes from the media, and civil society groups in Kashmir. It is largely based on the ecological and compensational resistance, not against the dispossession and displacement of the peasantry.

Chapter 7 and concluding chapter of the book explore the larger question of decision-makers, winners, and losers in this land-grabbing process. It explains the processes; who takes the decision, who owns what, who does what, who gets what and what do they do with it. After analysing these questions, the chapter ends with the concluding remarks about the whole land-grabbing process and argues that understanding the question of resistance, narratives, and overall land-grabbing in the fragile states, such as the conflict-hit region of Kashmir, needs an entire new framework, which theories about land-grabbing in normal regions do not offer.

2 Global Perspectives on Land-Grabbing

To contextualize land-grabbing in Kashmir within the global land-grabbing scenario, an attempt has been made here, to explore three major dimensions of the contemporary 'global land-grabbing'. The chapter begins with a discussion on the dominant assumptions about the current wave of land-grabbing; its features, impacts, and narratives. It then discusses property rights, actors, and power relations surrounding land-grabs and development-led dispossession and displacement. Moving on further, the chapter interrogates the literature on resistance towards land-grab, and discusses land-grabbing literature in India in particular. Finally, it provides concluding remarks about the existing literature on global land-grabs and how contemporary land-grab studies ignore this phenomenon of land-grab in conflict/disputed territories.

Global Land-Grabs: A Conceptual Debate

The phrase 'global land-grabbing' has been used to describe large-scale transnational land acquisitions and land deals that are taking place since 2008 food crisis. These land-grabs are carried for 'large scale-production, export of food and bio-fuels by companies or state-backed companies of south, mainly China, India, Gulf countries, and South Korea in the African continent to secure food for their own nations (Borras and Franco 2010; Cotula et al. 2009). Numerous scholars have, since then, examined the issue of land-grabbing from different perspectives. For example, De Schutter (2011) from a human rights perspective, Li (2011) from a labour perspective, Fairhead et al. (2012) from a political ecology perspective, White et al. (2012) from a political economy perspective, Borras et al. (2013) from a role of the state perspective, Mehta et al. (2012) from a water-grabbing perspective, and Margulis et al. (2013) from a globalization perspective. Besides the above-mentioned studies, there are several others, such as Borras and Franco (2010), World Bank (2010), Feldman and Geisler (2011), Levien (2013), and Rulli et al. (2013), which focus on the land and resource grabbing issue from diverse perspectives. Most of the above studies link the contemporary land-grabs to the 2007–8 food crisis, thereby underestimating the origin of land-grabs prior to 2008. This gap, however, was conversely filled with the Borras et al. (2012) study on Latin America, which not only questioned the dominant assumptions of land-grabbing and argued that land-grabbing in the region had started as early as 1990 but also described land-grabbing as actually being a 'control-grabbing' which infers power to control land and allied resources (Borras et al. 2012: 404). Simultaneously, Visser and Spoor's (2011) work on land-grabs in Soviet Eurasia, and Borras and Franco's (2011) study on land-grabs in South East Asia reshaped the debate on land-grabs, and added that they are not merely taking place in the African region, as was understood and projected by the scholars and NGOs till date, but this phenomenon was emerging in many regions of the world.

Most of these studies highlighted the various facets of contemporary land-grabs as a part of the neo-liberal economic order to control the land

and other resources of the people, which affects the livelihoods of rural peasantry, leads to displacement and dispossession, and causes ecological problems (Mishra 2011; Li 2011). Yet, other studies, for example the World Bank (2010) study, which is perhaps the most extensive study till date on global lands, acknowledged the existence of global land-grabs, and stressed on the point that land-grabs have taken place in countries where buyers could bribe the corrupt governments who lack capacity to regulate transactions. The World Bank study, however, sees the opportunity of productive investment in arable land to produce high yield, to fill what it calls 'yield gaps', and therefore provided seven guidelines—principles for responsible agriculture investment—or Principles for Responsible Agriculture Investment (RAI) principles, which it believed would help in fixing the deficiencies in land-grabs. Thus the report re-casted these land deals as an 'opportunity for the poor' in the form of bringing capitalist agro-industry in the rural areas, and allowing them to get the land on 'so called' win-win method, which could be achieved by applying the 'code of conduct' for land acquisition. However, the report has come under criticism (Borras and Franco 2010; De Schutter 2011; Li 2011) for giving sanction to large-scale land deals.

De Schutter's (2011) critique is based on the large-scale investment, which he sees not acceptable even if the investors follow the RAI principles. De Schutter's 'Minimum Human Rights Principles', which he proposed as UN Special Rapporteur, has been invoked by many NGOs, including La Via Campesina. Li (2011) on the other hand, is against the code of conduct to make the land deals 'pro-poor'. She stresses that it is the political mobilization and social struggles, not the regulatory measures, which have helped in safeguarding the interest of rural poor. Borras and Franco's (2010) study, on the other hand, provides a critique to the so called notion of marginalized land, and brands land classification as state's policy to control the spaces. Of course, Borras and Franco (2010) are not the first ones to highlight the state's role in classifying and declassifying land records to control land. Scott (1998) has much earlier pinpointed to this fact. However, Borras and Franco (2010) strengthen this argument in the context of contemporary land-grabs.

As the land-grabs become the 'catch-all' phrase for media and scholars, the literature creates a wedge whereby the data on land-grabs becomes questionable. Many scholars, lately though (Borras et al. 2012; Edelman 2013; Oya 2013), started questioning the data provided by many agencies/research institutes and argued that too much attention is paid on the scale of land deals. These scholars were obviously referring to Rulli et al. (2013) study, titled, 'Global Land and Water Grabbing' which claimed to be the most extensive study on land and water grabs, the World Bank (2010) study, which shows 45 million hectares have been grabbed, and OXFAM (2011) study which put the amount of global land-grabs as high as 227 million hectares. While Edelman stresses that there is a need of doing smaller ethnographic studies to understand the dynamics of land-grabbing, he argues, that so far, the data of larger studies has been questioned many times. Thus it becomes a challenge even for the researchers to justify real land-grabbing studies. Likewise, Oya, while acknowledging the contribution of grand studies in highlighting the phenomena of land-grabs, questions the larger studies, which are based on shaky data, and thus have policy implications. He argues that much of the land deals data is not known, and the data collected through satellites is not an effective way, as most of the times the satellite images of land are 'underutilized', 'marginal', and so on. This might not be the case when one sees it on the ground. Similarly, Edelman, points to the sources through which the data is collected, the reliability of sources, why the piece of information was revealed at a certain period of time and what are the underlying interests of the source to reveal the information. Thus, he argues for smaller studies while keeping historical background of the place in mind, which would give a thorough understanding of the land-grabs phenomena.

The literature on the impacts and features of land-grabbing is as varied as the assumptions and narratives about land-grabbing. Scores of studies have worked on the impacts of land-grabbing (Borras and Franco 2011, 2010; Bhaduri 2007; Li 2011; Mishra 2011). Looking at the question of contemporary land-grabbing, one of the main features of these land-grabs is that they are made in lieu of 'development'. Since the word 'development' is itself contested, nevertheless, these land-grabs are leading to a phenomenon of—development-induced displacement and dispossession. Many scholars (for example, Cernea 2007, 1997, 1990; Das 1996; Dwivedi 1997; Scudder 1991; Terminski 2013) have discussed in detail the issues arising due to development-induced displacement. At the same time the question of labour, and the dominant assumption that investment on land creates employment have been questioned by Tania Li (2011). Li argues that, since the governments of north subsidizes agriculture in their domestic countries, unlike the governments of southern countries, therefore, the governments of south encourage and 'supply land free to investors' to show increasing agriculture production which is presumed to create economic development. However, in reality it neither reduces poverty nor does it create employment. Li further argues that because of the very nature of the agro industry, of using high tech machines, it needs less labour, therefore creating a phenomenon where land is needed but not the labour.

Quite akin with Li's argument, Mishra (2011) in his study in Odisha (India) argues that the development projects for which the land was taken has failed to create any alternative livelihoods or employment for those who have been dispossessed and displaced. On similar lines, Bhaduri (2007) in his paper 'Alternatives in Industrialization' argues, that on the name industrialization is for 'common good', while landowners are being dispossessed and displaced, and their livelihoods are being snatched by transferring this land to corporations. Within this dynamics of dispossession, Mishra (2011) argues, that the phenomena of 'global land-grab' as part of globalization and neo-liberal economic systems has created many conflicts on water, land, and forests in the developing countries.

One the other hand, taking debate about the impact of land-grabs to an advanced level, De Schutter (2011) argues that, so far the debate about the 'global land-grab' has been confined to understand the impact on the dispossessed and displaced people. He further argues, that not enough has been done in understanding the impact of land-grabs on local farmers and other people who live besides the factories. These farmers not only have to compete with the big industries to sell their products, but often have to face several diseases because of smoke and dust, and see themselves as under-developed compared to the areas which are bought by corporations. Thus, land-grabbing has an impact even on the people who have not been dispossessed or displaced, however, they are affected due to the fact that they live near the industrial sector.

Actors, Power, and Politics in Land-Grabbing Debate

The role of actors in social science research, and specifically in rural development studies, has attracted attention of many scholars. Actor approach precisely focuses on the assumption that the 'actors interact and bargain with each other and thereby produce a policy outcome' (Mooij 2003). Long and Long (1992) stress on the agency of actors, with different interests, powers and resources, whose face-to-face interactions take place and bring out varied struggles and interactions among the individuals. Here the argument is made that the actors further forge alliances with others to mobilize support for their cause and interests. Thus, a concept of social interface is introduced. Long (1989) defines social interfaces as 'a critical point of intersection between different social systems, fields or levels of social order where structural discontinuities, based upon differences of normative value and social interest, are most likely to be found.' However, Biggs and Matsaert (2004) offer a word of caution, that given the heterogeneity of society where an individual has different political, religious, cultural, ethnic affiliations; therefore, the information should be used carefully, given the fact that the user cannot be called a neutral entity. Biggs and Matsaert warn that different actors might be affiliated with different political establishments, therefore information they give could be politically motivated. However, it is by examining and understanding perspectives of different actors, such as investors, state, civil society, peasants and others that we are able to better understand the complex topic of land politics.

As there are many actors involved in the land-grabbing debate, so researchers have focused on understanding the actors, and the power and politics surrounding the land-grabs phenomena. A sizable amount of literature (see, for example, Borras and Franco 2010; Borras et al. 2012;

Hall 2011; Lund 2011; Makki and Geisler 2011; OXFAM 2013; Schneider 2011) has been recently produced to understand the role of the state in land-grabs. Understating the role of state in land-grabbing, Makki and Geisler (2011) question the 'critical role of the state' in it. They argue that land-grabbing has to be looked through the prism of power dynamics vis-à-vis the role of the state in all these land deals. Likewise, Borras et al. (2013) explicitly explains how states facilitate land-grabs by way of; (*a*) 'invention/justification' of the need for large-scale land investments; (*b*) 'definition, reclassification and quantification' of what is 'marginal, under-utilized and empty' lands; (*c*) 'identification' of these particular types of land; (*d*) 'acquisition/appropriation' of these lands; and (*e*) 'reallocation/disposition' of these lands to investors. The question of reclassification of land as 'marginal' or 'wastelands' is also explained by Baka (2011) in her study on Tamil Nadu, India whereby the notion of 'wastelands' or 'marginal' land has been used for the perception management of converting agriculture land into real estate. State has been found using extra-economic coercion against the unarmed people who protest against dispossession and displacement (Das 2011). Likewise, Mishra (2011) has found in his study on Odisha, that people have often protested against the use of 'state power' which facilitated land-grabs in the region. These protests are being handled with an iron fist by the state to facilitate bad land deals. What is important to note here, is that, what has been forgotten is what De Schutter (2011) calls 'cultural significance' of the land and Scott (1976) calls 'social functions' of the land. Prior to De Schutter and Scott, Karl Polanyi (1944) highlighted decades earlier, that natural resources such as land and water are just treated as economic resources. This very nature of treating land as an economic asset, while denouncing feeling, emotions, status, and security attached to it, often makes people protest against the same land. State power and state's role in the development process can be further looked into from the state's role in facilitating these grabs (Bardhan 1998; Wade 1985).

Besides state, it is the corporates that are the major or primary actors of land-grabbing. In almost all the above mentioned studies, and other studies (like Borras and Franco 2010; De Schutter 2011;

GRAIN 2008; Mishra 2011; OXFAM 2013; Schneider 2011; World Bank 2010); have majorly focused on the role of corporates in land-grabbing. The corporate/capital or The Transnational Institute arguments stated in the World Bank report (2010) frames these land deals as a win-win deal for the buyers and sellers, which can create economic development and employment in the host country. However, as mentioned above, Li (2011) rejects both the notions.

At the same time, the World Bank (2010) and De Schutter (2011) have noticed that there are instances where corporates bribe the governments to get the land deals done. The OXFAM (2013: 4) study stresses 'that investors actively target countries with weak governance in order to maximise profits and minimise red tape'. Thus, the OXFAM (2013) study follows a similar line as many other scholars who stress on land rights and land reforms, and believe in securing land rights as a means to end the land-grabs issue. For example, Cotula et al. (2009) mention in their study on 'Land-grab or development opportunity' that there are weaknesses in the national laws of many countries for the local people, thus there is a need for strengthening laws for them. The wider debate is to secure the rights of local people who face the brunt of all these land deals. While in some places these rights are defined, however, just on paper, but in other places, laws of development for the local people, which secure and preserve the local culture, identity, and livelihoods do not even exist. However, as Borras and Franco (2012) observe, land-grabbing is also taking place in India, Philippines, Brazil, and other countries, where land reforms have already taken place. Moreover, land reforms theoretically entail land redistributing 'land ownership from large private landowners to small peasant farmers and landless agricultural workers' (Griffin et al. 2002: 279–80). However, most of the land-grabs are not private lands but state, forest, and other lands, and therefore outside the permit of conventional land-grabs (Borras and Franco 2012). Therefore, just securing the land rights would not solve the land-grabbing issue. Similarly Levien (2013) in his study on SEZs in India has observed how corporate land deals lead to dispossession and displacement, and at the same time how state has just become a land broker by transferring land from (or to) capitalist firms that has resulted in land wars in the country. The application of the similar concern, as well as power relations, which included bribing the government employees and politicians by the investors to get the benefits, has become the subject of many studies and appeared in many newspaper headlines recently. However, while analysing the actors, and power relations in land politics, it is important to note that power here does not have to be looked through the 'hegemonic control, the hierarchy, capacity to act', and the position one holds in government or elsewhere, rather power has to be seen through the social status, reputation, educational level, the capacity to resist and negotiate (Long 2001).

Global Land-Grabs and the Question of Resistance

When one looks at the literature on land-grabs and resistance, there are quite a few studies available on resistance to 'global land-grabs'. However, the question of resistance in peasant societies, agrarian movements, political problems, and other socio political and economic issue have been dealt in length and breadth in the academic studies (Kerkvliet 2009; Scott 1998, 1985, 1976; Wolf 1969).

Here Lasswell's (1958) definition of politics—who gets what, when, and how—serves the purpose of understating the question of resistance. This can be further linked to the argument put forward by Kerkvliet (2009), which stresses on understanding resistance through political structure. Thus, Kerkvliet argues that the question of resistance cannot be understood without understanding the political structure of the system in which resistance occurs; and politics as elaborated by him is about 'control, allocation, production and use of resources and values and ideas underlying those resources' (2009: 230). Foucault (1978: 93) saw the resistance as an essential element to counter the power; thus arguing, 'Where there is power, there is resistance'. While Foucault is believed to be an inspiration for resistance studies and subaltern studies, however, it is Fanon, alongside some other western leftist scholars, such as Sartre, who propagated active resistance and provided intellectual support to the peasant movement in 1950s.

Resistance has been defined and conceptualized by many theorists. Borras and Franco (2013) identified three important contestations around current land-grabbing: poor people versus the corporate, poor people versus the state, and poor people versus poor people. While poor people versus corporate is a fight for remuneration, more compensation, employment, scholarships, and so on, poor people versus the state is about expulsion and relocation and resettlements. Poor people versus poor people is the inter and intra-class fight (Borras and Franco 2013). Seymour (2006) defines resistance as 'intentional, and hence conscious, acts of defiance or opposition by a subordinate individual or group of individuals against a superior individual or group of individuals' (Seymour 2006: 305). Therefore, the stress is given on the 'conscious resistance' by Seymour. As per his notion of resistance any act of resistance which is not 'conscious' may not be called resistance. However, it is hard to judge when a person is consciously taking decision and when he/she is not. Are all the resisting population/people conscious about their rights or injustice, while others are not? These are the questions, which need to be looked in details.

Seymour (2006) further offers a critique on theorizing resistance in the cultural anthropology perspective. He goes on to argue that part of the problem in theorizing resistance is because of the anti-psychological position taken by the resistance theorists. Thus, he argues that, it would not be possible to understand the resistance unless we understand what motivates people to resist, which is linked to the 'internalized cultural motivation' which persuades or motivates these actions. Seymour applies psychological anthropology perspective to three ethnographies of resistance in South and South East Asia, and argues that either the acts are not resistance or they are not understood through psychological anthropology perspective which understands 'intentionality' of actor's defiance of coercive institutions.

James Scott (1985), perhaps one of the most influential theorist on peasant resistance in the present time, in his in-depth and valuable study in Malaysia titled *Weapons of the Weak*, argues that it is the everyday struggles of collective individuals which help them (peasants) to achieve their goal, than occasional episodes and rebellions. However, Scott has been criticized by Walker (2008) for projecting or defining peasants as defensive and disempowered who are not able to change their conditions.

Following the path of Scott in understanding resistance, Kerkvliet (2009) in his study 'Everyday politics of peasants (and ours)' discuss the everyday politics of peasants. The study is very important in the context to understand the peasant resistance. Kerkvliet builds upon Scott's theory and takes us to understand how people contest, accept, challenge, and adjust with the existing norms 'over the allocation of resources'. They do it by a subtle and mundane, however, often unorganized way to get their demands met. Unlike official and advocacy politics—the two other forms of peasant politics—the people who do everyday politics do not know they are doing politics, with no organization structure in place. While, Kerkvliet has explained and theorized the concept of politics in the peasant societies and the ways and forms of resistance; he, however, ignores to understand these village and peasant societies in a holistic manner when he says they are not organized. Village forms of life may not be organized according to present day management ways, but villages have their own structure and organization which often works on verbal laws/ways of village, rather than, some defined ones. The respect and obedience to the elders is one of them, where an elder can ask the whole village to gather for the common good. It is abided by one and all. The elder or head of the village might not be a chosen or an elite one, selected because of his/her wealth or power, but by his association and respect due to his conduct and contribution in the development of the village. However, Kerkvliet goes on to explain that peasants sometimes use different forms of resistance like official advocacy politics, which is often organized, structured, and overt; or everyday resistance/politics which is unorganized, unstructured, and covert. Drawing on everyday forms of resistance, Adnan (2007) argues in his study on Bangladesh, that if the political systems tend to favour individuals and institutions, this can push peasants to 'cross the threshold of fear and insecurity'.

On the other hand, O'Brien and Li (2006) in their study on peasant resistance in China offer a very interesting variant of Scott and Kerkvliet's work, which came to be known as 'rightful resistance'. They argue that peasants invoke the promises made by the leaders and the constitutional laws to demand their rights through unstructured and unorganized means in the way that Scott and Kerkvleit saw everyday peasant politics, which is not a covert but an overt resistance. While the everyday forms of resistance was observed as disguised, anonymous, quiet and mundane, rightful resistance was described as more open, public, and noisy (O'Brien 2013).

Explaining the resistance to current wave of land-grabbing, Li (2011) underlines that there are two waves of resistance against the current global land-grabs; while some fight against the land-grabs, others fight for compensation. Schneider (2011) in his study on land-grab and resistance in rural Cambodia depicts the tale of how the state forcibly acquired land for the corporates and how people responded to these land acquisitions by graduating their resistance from everyday rightful resistance to overt forms of resistance.

Though Schneider (2011) gives a detailed account on the resistance through political economic perspective and also applies Scott and Kerkvliet's perspective of everyday politics, however, he fails to theorize the forms and means of protests—why some resist while others do not.

On the other hand, Kumar (2011) in his work on land acquisition in special economic zone of India, digs on the flaws of land laws and argues that the law of the land in India allows resistance in the matter of compensation only. People cannot refuse to give land, however, they can resist/demand for more compensation. Therefore, it goes on similar lines with Li (2011), who sees resistance for compensation as one of the means of resistance against land-grabs.

Makki and Geisler (2011) argue that the present wave of complex resistance will reshape and offer a challenge to the neoliberal doctrines which have over the years defined economic and political systems on the basis of its ideological base. Thus the problem of economic crisis which the pundits of the neoliberal project have tried or are trying to solve by 'the extension of market relations' has/is facing stiff resistance. This becomes more challenging to understand whether the neo-liberal policies of emergence of industrial capitalism in rural societies will change livelihoods structure, lead forced commoditization—thus merge with capitalist economy, or the resistance movements will force industrial capitalism project to mend its ways and thinking about expansion and henceforth, the idea of development. It might happen, as peasants might like to absorb both the forms of development—industrial as well as agro-based—for the rural areas. Bardhan (2011) argues, that the Gandhian critics have not shown any sustainable alternative to industrial capitalism, which would work for the development of large population like India. However, Gandhian and leftist ideologues are 'hunting India' and have started a staunch attack on Indian government for its neo-liberal economic policies. Thus he argues, most of the Indians are against the anti-market and anti-capitalist. This might be too far in thinking, as the protests on the streets might not often reflect rejection or condemnation of capitalist development, but rather these protests will strengthen the democracy, and therefore, can reshape the capitalist thinking towards pro-people development, which might be acceptable to one and all.

Ortner (1995: 183) stresses on the resistance studies to understand the resistance through consciousness, subjectivity, intentionality, and identity. Therefore, Ortner's perspective hints towards partly applying the psychological anthropological perspective. However, his perspective has been criticized for just re-examining the concept of power (Seymour 2006). The study becomes a good lead in understanding the motivation of resistance. The concept is then further taken by Fletcher (2010) in his study titled 'What Are We Fighting For? Rethinking Resistance in a Pewenche Community in Chile', in which he argues why some people resisted relocation for the dam construction while others did not. However, his argument is misleading as it only examines the power relations, and does not apply psychological anthropological perspective in understanding the resistance (Seymour 2006). Though Fletcher attempts to go beyond Scott's theory of resistance, however, he fails not only in understanding psychological analysis as noted by Seymour, but also to do justice either with power dynamic of resistance by analysing it through class dynamics, and cultural influence of individual's behaviour through cultural anthropology perspective.

There has been a debate on whether all the farmers are against land acquisition or against the ways in which land acquisition is carried out. Nielsen (2010) in his study on 'Contesting India's Development/ Industrialization, Land Acquisition and Protest in West Bengal', emphasizes that farmers in Singur were not by and large against the Tata Motors project or industrialization. They wanted industrialization, however, they were against the concept of converting farmland into industrial land and taking land forcibly from small farmers without acquiring proper consent from them during the land acquisition process. Their aim or desire was to have both agricultural sources of employment as well as industrial system of employment available with them. Thus converting farmland would not go in their interest. Nielson further argues that the main groups who would criticize the neo-liberal model of development in Singur were NGOs, activists, and political organizations. The joining of NGOs and activist groups with the farmers not only forced the Tatas to leave Singur, but made the Left-leaning Government of West Bengal lose its election and power after 35 years of continuous rule. Likewise, Nyari (2008) also discusses the support of village level NGO in Ghana against the land-grab for biofuel, which has played an important role in addressing the land issue. Thus, role of civil society actors, transnational agrarian movements, and media becomes very important in understanding the resistance to the contemporary land deals.

Within this huge body of literature on resistance against land-grabs, struggles of peasants, and marginalized groups in different parts of the world, very negligible amount of work has been produced on resistance against land-grabs in conflict zones or disputed territories. Nevertheless, scholarship on land politics, dispossession, and displacement in Palestine provides a very interesting account of forms of resistance offered by Palestinian people against the land control (Cohen 2000; Fischbach 2003; Forman and Kedar 2004; Golan 2001; Peretz 1958). Salih and Sophie's (2014) work 'Cultures of Resistance in Palestine and Beyond: One the Politics of Art, Aesthetics and Affect' and Forman and Kedar's (2004) work 'From Arab land to "Israel Lands": The Legal Dispossession of the Palestinians Displaced by Israel in the wake of 1948' gives us a textual view of how dispossession of Palestine Arabs, displaced in 1948 war (referred to by Israelis as the 'War of Independence' and by Palestinians as 'the Catastrophe'), has become an Israeli state policy. Here the law is being used, first to institutionalize the dispossession of Palestinian and then integrate their land into the new system of 'Jewish National Land'. Salih and Sophie argue that the Palestine land is also deemed as a 'vital resource for securing Israeli state interests.' To justify the control on land as 'legitimate', Israeli state has been using rule of law for either affecting or normalizing the outcome (Forman and Kedar 2004). Thus, occupation of land in Israel state's view becomes important to serve the Israeli National Interest. Within this occupation and resistance, new forms of art resistance against dispossession by young Palestinians have emerged and are going beyond Palestinian 'classical' art forms: Mehmoud Darwish's poetry, Suleiman Manshour's paintings, and Kanafani's literature to express their resistance against land and now presenting resistance through 'Rap music' (Forman and Kedar 2004).

No doubt state directed violence is pervasive in conflict zones, but of late, modern market economies venturing into traditional peasant life and extraction of the peasants resources are responsible for rebellions in many parts of the world (Desai and Eckstein 1990). For example, Nayak's (2015) work, 'Development Induced Displacement and Arms Conflicts in Bangladesh', explains how Bangladesh's Chittagong (CHT) area has been facing armed insurgency since 1950, after tens of thousands of tribal people were displaced due to the Kaptai Hydroelectricity Project in 1957. Since then tribals have been at the receiving end of state violence. Tribal people, who got displaced due to hydroelectricity project, were in certain cases paid no compensation due to the absence of land rights or were given minimum compensation; at the same time these projects did not help them in any way, rather led to their displacement either inside Bangladesh or outside the country to neighbouring India. Many displaced peasants launched an armed resistance against the state for snatching CHT's autonomous rights, resources' extraction and the permanent settlement of non-tribal people in the tribal areas. It was also against the displacement and the worsening conditions of the displaced populace as well as the absence of the government for the proper addressal of their grievances. Instead of giving them autonomy, state scrapped the special laws which protected them, in order to bring these people under the so-called national system. Besides demographic change through settlement of external population to avoid 'threat to National Security'; in the present times neo-liberal capital has ventured in the area taking the resources away from the region and leading to forced commoditization (Nayak 2015). Like Bangladesh, there are similar or more severe cases of conflict over land in many regions in India, Pakistan, Sri Lanka and few other south and south east countries where there are organized resistance movements, such as Naxalites in Central India, Tamils in Sri Lanka or unorganized, mundane or passive resistance groups in Indian Administered Kashmir, Baluchistan, Khyber Pakhtunkha, Pakistani administered Kashmir, in Pakistan and Xinijang, and Tibet in China (Adnan 2014; Baviskar 2008; Ballard 1991; Bendfeldt 2010; Joanne 2013; Peer and Ye 2015; Roy 2010; Sundar 2007). Resistance in conflict zones thus require what Adnan Shapan emphasizes as understanding the political structure in which the resistances occur. And different forms such overt, covert or both forms of resistance sometimes leading to armed insurgency, rebellions, and so on, would primarily depend on structure of domination in which the peasantry is living and the means and institutions of resistance that are available to them (Adnan 2011).

Land-Grabs in India

Land-grabs in India are largely considered as post reform phenomena, ignoring the predations of such state assisted entities as the East India Company, and refer to the economic reforms that took place when India liberalized its economy in 1991. This meant opening its economy to foreign direct investment, by multinational companies, as well as encouraging national companies to invest in the Indian market (Bhaduri 2007; Sampat 2010). With the opening of Indian economy and subsequent establishment of SEZs, scholars, media, and

NGOs published loads of literature on SEZs, their impacts, and benefits on the people and India. Numerous studies (Baka 2011; Balakrishnan 2012; Bhaduri 2007; Kumar 2011; Levien 2013, 2011; Mahalingam and Vyas 2011; Mishra 2011; Sampat 2010) have discussed the land-grabs in India, but mostly focused on SEZs. Levien argues that land-grabs in India have to be looked through India's historical context, which included dispossession due to railways, forest enclosures by British Raj or later after independence dispossessions due to Nehruvian state-led development model (2013: 381). In the present context, Mujumder's (2010) study on 'Nano' project in West Bengal, puts light on how Indian states are competing for getting investment, and on the peasant struggles around these lands. Thus he argues that the question of land should not be understood through its market value or exchange value, rather there are complex realities and relationships surrounding the land, which need to be taken into consideration. What is more is that the responses to the land-grabs have to be looked by understanding these complexities and contradictions, which are embedded in a given political and social system.

In her study on SEZs in India, Sampat (2010) argues, how establishment of the SEZs in different states has become the reason for displacement of thousands of peasants, while providing land to the neo-liberal corporations. Similar line is echoed in the Levien (2011) and Kumar (2011) studies, both of which argue that by virtue of the state having sole power to acquire the land, and transfer the same to the private corporations, it has resulted in displacement of the peasants, and caused land wars in the country (Levien 2013). Thus Lahiri-Dutt et al. (2012) make an argument that the existing laws in mining areas need to be modified and strengthened to support the local people to share the benefit.

Making the support for capital-led development, Tyagi et al. (2007) ardently argued for the expansion of SEZs in India, which they believe would create employment and development in the country. Tyagi et al., further argue that the size of SEZs should be expanded as well as the infrastructure such as, roads, ports, among others, around these SEZs, should be developed on the pattern of China, which would boost the Indian economy. Providing critique to those who put on emphasis on agriculture-based development, they argue, urbanization and industrialization are the main drivers of development, therefore agriculture should not become roadblock in that process.

As we closely look at the literature on the land-grabs and displacement and dispossession caused by Nehruvian concept of state-sponsored model, we do not see much of the literature on it, it is perhaps due to the reason what Guha (2008: 224) believes that there was an 'overwhelming consensus in favour of a heavy industry-oriented, state-supported model of development', which gave legitimacy to the projects like dams. Nonetheless, Roy (2007) points out it should be interrogated whether this 'consensus' was among those who were affected due to these projects or not? It is however to be noted that there were instances of resistance (unsuccessful though) against the dams (Guha 2008; Levien 2013; Parry and Struempell 2008), and these protests spread later in post 1990s.

***

Examining the existing literature on global land for water grabs, I started with the understanding of looking at the questions of the meanings, assumptions, features, and actors of the current wave of land-grabs. What I have found is that too much emphasis is given on the quantification of the land-grabs, and too much emphasis is put on the land-grabs in a special region. Moreover, existing literature explores the role of different actors, especially the state, corporates, and other powerhouses—including institutions and elites in land deals. The question of power dynamics of these land-grabs brings the resistance to these land-grabs. However, most of the literatures miss the link between the political structure and resistance. Under what circumstances resistance is possible and under what circumstances it is not. While a sizeable literature talks about the land-grabs in India, however, most of this literature focuses on SEZs, thus forgets or ignores the land-grabs led by the state agencies/corporations.

Moreover, the literature on peasant resistance in general focuses on and explains peasants as a monolithic community aloof from other identities, however, peasants in India, and in Kashmir in particular, do not see themselves only as a certain community affected by the larger community, but part of the nation in case of India, and part of the larger Kashmiri community, in case of Kashmir, who are fighting for the larger cause (see further discussion on multiple identities of Kashmiri peasants in Chapters 4, 5, and 6).

3   Political and Economic History of Land-Grabs in India

In understanding a subject or a phenomena, the biggest question one faces is how much historical background of a certain phenomenon is sufficient to explain it. The question becomes more difficult when one tries to understand the question of land politics. This is so because land is not only an embodiment of mineral resources, a location for habitation, a place for work but also a predominant source for food and, therefore, obviously, a complex topic to deal with. Since the subject of this work is to understand land-grabbing by a state corporation, it is fair to go back to the historical roots of land-grabbing in India. And understanding that phenomena entails simply to understand the resource-grabbing in India historically. By so doing we will also understand the similarities and dissimilarities of contemporary land-grabs with the land acquisitions that were done in earlier regimes. This will also help us to understand how land-grabs in Kashmir has a pattern similar to that of land-grabs in the rest of India.

This chapter therefore begins with tracing the roots of colonialism in India followed by understanding its various structures and the process of resource-grabbing. It moves on to highlight the response of the Indian society to colonialism and underlines the legacies of colonialism with a purpose to understand the developmental policy—issues and concerns— of independent India. Nevertheless, this chapter also attempts to understand the underlying factors which forced the Indian state, initially to bring under its own control various resources and means of production, and later to adopt measures to liberalize the economy. These processes helped India move towards a development path, however, this period marked an era, where land was neglected over 'Temples of India'—dams and steel plants. Last but not the least, the chapter also tries to place the question of economic exploitation of Kashmir via land and water-grab in the context of India's growing energy deficits.

Colonization, Resource Extraction/Exploitation, and Peasant Response

During the ancient and medieval times India was ruled by foreigners at different points of time. However, it was during the eighteenth century, when British rule was founded, that India became a colonized land. Unlike the earlier foreign rulers the British did not make India their home and instead exploited its resources for their own betterment in India and abroad. It would not be out of place to mention that the rulers, other than the British, spent the wealth generated through taxation and otherwise within India whereas from the very beginning the British considered India a foreign land and its people, the 'other'. India was made to serve as an engine of revenue and its wealth was drained to England without any breaks. The mechanism of the 'Drain of Wealth' however changed with the changing nature of colonialism. Since the British empire emerged from the ruins of the Mughal empire and was brought into existence by a trading company with profit as a paramount driving force, therefore, for a considerable period of time the system of administration and governance put in place was to a large extent based on the Mughal System of Governance—its institutions and administrative machinery. It is therefore important to briefly discuss land-relations in India during the Mughal period so as to understand the changes introduced under colonialism, which in turn would help in understanding the politics around land and other natural resources in independent India.

The Mughal dynasty rule, which began in 1526 with the conquest of India by its first conqueror Babar, set a precedent of benevolence towards its subjects, which was followed by his heirs: Humayun, Akbar, Jahangir, and Shah Jahan until Aurangzeb. Alexener Dow, who sees great wisdom and governance skills among Mughal kings, describes Mughal rule thus:

> The uncommon abilities of most of the princes, with mild and humane character of all, rendered Hindostan the most flourishing empire in the world during two complete centuries. The manly and generous temper of Baber permitted not oppression to attend the victories of hid sword .... Humaioon, though not equal in abilities to his father, carried all his mild virtues into the throne ... Akbar was possessed of Baber's intrepidity in war, of Humaioon's mildness in peace ... Jahangire ... was the invariable protector of the people against the rapacity and tyranny of his own officers ... His son, Shah Jahan ... rendered his people happy by gravity, justice and solemnity of his decisions ... Aurangzebe ... kept the great machine of government in motion through all its members: his penetrating eye followed oppression to its most secret retreats, and his stern justice established tranquility, and secured property over all his extensive dominions. (Alexener Dow, cited in Guha 1996: 30)

Tolerance and Mughal rulers as highlighted by Ranajit Guha (1996) and emphasized by Sen (1999) in his thought-provoking work, *Development as Freedom*, whereby he argues that Mughal rulers were more tolerant and had a great respect of human rights, including the respect of choosing or disowning ones religion, than their contemporaries in Europe. Mughal benevolence towards their subjects was drawn from the fact that they knew that their strengths lie on the prosperity of their subjects (Guha 1996). Therefore, unlike their predecessors Turco-Afghans, and Pathans, which Dow describes as tyrannical, Mughals on the other hand, built roads, infrastructure, commerce, agriculture, and so on.

While Mughals did infrastructure development, they, at the same time did impose some taxes on their subjects to generate revenue. However, what is important to note here is that land was less important than labour in Mughal period and early British period, as the available land mass in the entire Indian subcontinent was much more than what was required to fulfil the requirements of people. The importance of land in economic terms was only felt when British introduced the concept of private property in the region (Whitehead and Locke 2011). However, it was the Mughals who did land categorization in India and British followed the same landlord—peasant relationship, with stringent means.

Therefore, in order to understand the resource extraction in Kashmir by NHPC it would be extremely significant and insightful to understand the mechanisms and methods of resource extraction adopted by the English East India Company in India (henceforth EIC). It is pertinent to note that though EIC did not bring India under foreign rule for the first time, however, it was under their rule that India's resources were exploited in an organized manner for the profit/advantage of people beyond India's political boundaries. It is for the same reason that a considerable section of Kashmir society considers NHPC as a new brand of EIC. In the present study while as no such attempt of comparison is made, understanding the history of land and water-grabbing or resource-grabbing by East India company would give us an idea about the Indian people's struggle against the resource exploitation in the first place, and the impact of British imperialism in the later stages.

No doubt the arguments of the imperial apologists that India had a closed type of economy prior to the establishment of British rule, devoid of the concept of private property, has been adequately contested by the nationalists and other scholars, however, there is no denying the fact that during the British rule the Indian economy was integrated with the global economy on a larger scale. This was facilitated initially by the EIC which considered its trade interests paramount to all other interests, often resorting to force as axiom of trade. By using its trading monopoly and political authority in India the company started an era of exploitation characterized by what came to be known as the Drain of Wealth. The global demand for Indian goods was met through the unilateral transfer of Indian goods to the markets in the west. It is worth mentioning that the Indian goods were purchased by making use of the revenues appropriated from the Indian peasants. The integration of Indian economy with the world economy became more intense with the industrial revolution in England and subsequent opening of Indian economy to free trade. It is pertinent to mention that this economic integration not only ruined the Indian handicrafts by exposing them to severe external competition without any protection but also subjected the Indian peasant to the influence of market swings outside India. This was so because of commercial orientation of Indian agriculture. The underlying feature of this economic integration however, was to make the Indian economy subservient to the British Economy. Even after the transfer of power to the British crown, the Indian economy continued to be subservient to the British economy. In fact it was after AD 1858 that a classical colonial type of relation took concrete form.

For the purpose of achieving their set goals—initially to appropriate as much of land revenue as possible to invest the same for the purchase of Indian exportable goods, and later to promote agriculture for feeding raw material to British industries—the British introduced changes in the Indian agrarian structure at different points of time. The first such change was introduced through the permanent settlement of Bengal in AD 1793 under which the concept of private property was introduced. Later on the British also paved way for commercialization of agriculture, though not an unforced one. Thus, under the British, Indian economy always worked as a subordinate economy with its land, the main source of economy, and forest resources, always used by the British to serve their own purposes.

The imposition of extraordinary taxes on the peasantry and working class, besides exploitation of India's natural resources during colonial period has become the subject of many studies (Chatterjee

1993; Chunder 1904; Guha 1999; Manikumar 2003). The economic historians have described this phase as the worst phase of Indian history, in which India's raw materials, gold and other monuments were transported to Britain, and in return Indians were systematically forced to buy the finished products for exorbitant prizes. It is important to mention here that, the expansion of the company and colonization was only possible with the emergence of modern technology, especially railways, which facilitated transportation of extracted goods from one place to the other. As Guha (2006: 8) observes, 'railway, for example, came to India in less than two decades after its invention in Britain. By 1900 there were more than 30,000 sq. miles of tracks in the Indian subcontinent.' The construction of railways and mining caused cutting down and destruction of thousands of miles of forest area, and displaced people from their native places (Guha 2006: 8).

In response to the imposition of exorbitant taxes to the peasantry class, and extortion and use of brutal force to rest of the community, there were many resistance movements against the company. While most of the times, flight was chosen as a weapon, as the land was not seen as important as the labour; however, the extraction of resources from the company and exploitation of labour and peasantry had gained steam in resistance, which lead to emergence of a number of peasant movements across the region (Guha 1999). The agrarian society in India has experienced several peasant movements; the Malabar peasant struggle in the early 20th century, the peasant struggle in Oudh in the 1920s and 1930s, the Tebhaga movement in Bengal in 1946–47, the Telangana movement in Andhra Pradesh in 1948–52 and the Naxalite movement during 1967–71 in West Bengal, Bihar, Andhra Pradesh and some other states' (Debal and Singha 2004: 32), and the Chipko movement in early 1970s (Guha 2006), and other smaller or bigger movements, some noticed, while others not, remained firm in fighting against the Raj or Independent Indian state.

Land Acquisition: A Colonial Legacy

A sizable amount of literature (Bose 2008; Chatterjee 1993; Guha 2006, 1999, 1996; Mukherjee 2004; Whitehead and Locke 2011) offers critique on the EIC-led colonization in India, which is primarily seen through the lens of imperialism, whereby the company extracted Indian resources, exploiting labour to produce these resources and then supplying them to Britain. The exploitation of resources and control of land and labour during the colonial period has been a proven fact by the scholars; nonetheless, colonization served or paved way for the institutional and infrastructural development in India as well. As Scott (1976) notes, while the establishment of railways created a means to transport the resources from one area to the other, at the same time, it helped to supply the food to the areas, which were facing food scarcity, thus helping to avoid famine to a certain extent.

Understanding colonial period vis-à-vis present time governance system is also important in this context because even after Independence, the laws enacted during the colonial times, were/are pretty much still functional or were adopted after the British left India. For example, the Land Acquisition Act of 1894, which allowed the state and railways to take land, was functional for ninety years, and this was modified in 1984, when amendments were made to this Act, which allowed governments to take land for any public purpose. While the 1894 Act was deficient in having provisions for relief and rehabilitation of those who are affected, at the same time the meaning of public purpose was kept so vague that the government could acquire land for and with any motive under the guise of 'public purpose'. However, what is interesting is the amendment made to the Act of 1984, of course this time, under Independent India's Congress rule. The new amendments allowed rampant use of land acquisition, in the name of 'public purpose', most of the times directly to gain the access the land for private players for public-private partnership.

It is worthy here to stretch a bit back and understand the question and definition of land and the concept of privatization of land, which allows us to understand why land was taken in colonial period, and how it is still relevant. It was the British who introduced the concept of private property in India. The very process led to the control of open spaces, forest areas, agricultural land, marshland, grassland, and so on by the government for the market forces. This was done, as Whitehead and Locke (2011) argue, under the influence of John Locke's labour theory of property. 'Arguing that a "state of nature" and "wilde woods" could still be found in America in the 1600s, Locke maintained that by enclosing such lands and bringing them under intensive cultivation, English colonisation of the Americas would raise global agricultural productivity and provide a source of increased trade from which all populations would benefit' (Whitehead and Locke 2011: 2). The British followed a similar pattern here by controlling forests and other lands through revenue settlements and forest laws (Guha 1996; Wells 2007). This very classification of land, under which the community lands where described as 'waste' lands in Lockian terms, and needed to be brought under cultivation together with other lands which were not seen as economically productive, in Smith's definition of 'productive' and 'unproductive'. Therefore control of the lands for the 'productive' purposes was seen necessary. The categorization of lands as marsh land, unused land, unproductive land, and so on, together with the laws through which these lands are being controlled are still prevalent in India; therefore play a crucial role in land and resource politics today.

Nonetheless, in September 2013, the Indian Parliament passed a new land acquisition bill, named as Land Acquisition and Rehabilitation Act, 2013, which addressed many concerns of the land acquisition process, (party) the definition of public purpose, however, leaves the question of categorization of land unanswered. We shall discuss the new land acquisition bill in the next section.

India: From Swadeshi to Liberalization and the Question of Land

With some features from the US democratic system, and most of the features from British political and administrative system, India, with a slight modification, created its own democracy and administrative system after 1947 (Map 3.1). Without compromising on its promises and commitments, the Indian National Congress not only devised a program for the abolition of landlordism but also nationalized some of the very important resources of the country. This brought into existence a mixed type of economy with features of both—capitalistic and socialistic systems.

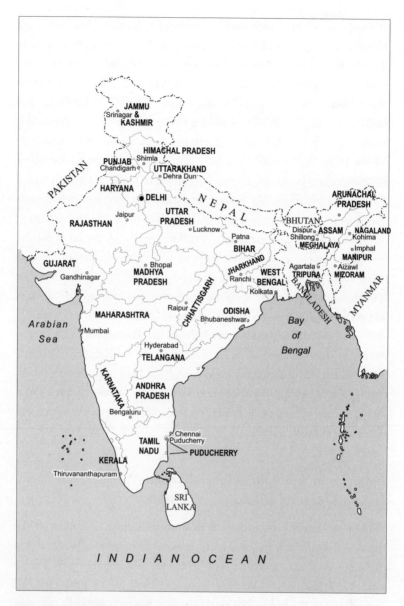

Map 3.1   Map of India

Source: Based on resources from India Maps.

Note: This map is not to scale and does not depict authentic political boundaries.

Almost all the sectors, including banking, industries, and so on, were brought under the government's control. The government on the one hand controlled these sectors; and on the other hand, it planned a state led development in rural India. In fact the Second Five-Year Plan (1956–61) stressed on rural development through industrial development, which included development of steal plants, dams, and hydroelectricity projects to promote local development, away from the dependence of foreign powers (Parry and Struempell 2008; Vietor 2007). Gandhi's slogan of Swadeshi and 'buy Indian' was implemented and propagated (partly though) by socialist Jawaharlal Nehru. In fact import substitution policy was the hallmark of the Nehruvian phase and continued with slight modifications up to the late 1970s. Driven by the desire to achieve self-sufficiency in agriculture and manufacturing sectors the state initiated a process of rural transformation together with establishment of what came to be called the 'Temples of India'—dams and steel plants. The Nehruvian era witnessed the creation of steel plants, hydroelectricity projects, dams, and to some extent, roads. This period, from 1947 to early 1970, was however a period of indifference towards the ecology. Guha (2006) describes this period as that of 'ecological innocence' whereby catching up with the developed nations was kept as a motive; and land, environment, and peasant concerns were neglected over the 'Temples of India'. Nehru's obsession with dams and steel plants led to the creation of dams for irrigation and for hydroelectricity generation all over India. As per National Register of Large Dams 2016—the latest government data available on dams—there exist 4,877 large national dams and 313 large dams are under construction in the country (NRLD 2016). While most of the dams are constructed and maintained by the state governments, there are few constructed by corporations, which includes, NHPC, the corporation under study.

Nonetheless, there were some resistant movements witnessed against the dams, but their footprints were not so dominant (Levien 2013). The construction of these large dams, such as Bhakra Nangal Dam, Narmada Valley, Silent Valley, Damodar Valley, and so on, was projected to solve the problems of water scarcity, in terms of irrigation and drinking water, and solve the energy crisis, by building HEPs.

During the times of Indira Gandhi, the Prime Minister of India from 1980–4, there was not much change in terms of development model and government control and restrictions on licensing to run business continued. However, 'in 1973, Indira Gandhi got the Parliament to enact the Foreign Exchange Regulation Act, which allowed 40 per cent limit on foreign equity ownership' (Vietor 2007: 90). It was a big leap forward from her father's controlled policy towards the policy of selective liberalization; which Gandhi felt is necessary to control inflation and decline in foreign exchange reserves. As Dash (1999: 891) observes, Indira Gandhi took two important decisions to combat this economic problem: one, she went for selective liberalization and the second, she applied for a loan to International Monetary Fund (IMF). Even though she was attacked by her opponents like Bharatiya Janata Party (BJP) and Communist Party for giving up Swadeshi policy, nonetheless, her substantial majority in the Lower House of the Parliament gave her the authority and legitimacy to stick to her stand.

Not paying any heed to the opposition parties such as the BJP and Communist party, Gandhi applied for a loan from the IMF. She was proved right when she was granted the loan in 1981 by IMF, and had got backing from the business sections of India. On top of that, India was able to pay all of the loan back to IMF by 1984 (Vandana 2008). Indira Gandhi's move for seeking help from IMF happened in the backdrop of an oil crisis due to an agitation in the oil producing state of Assam, a draught causing a 15 per cent decline in agriculture production, and the very existence of regulated transportation, subsidizing fertilizers, and support to the companies or 'sick units'[1] which caused a huge amount of the money to the

---

[1] 'Sick units' were the companies which would go bankrupt. The state would support them through state-owned banks. Richard (2007) mentions, that in 1980s there were more than ninety thousand 'sick units'. These 'sick units' could not easily layoff employees, because around hundred government rules would not accept the financial difficulty of a company to layoff its employees.

state exchequer. While India was able to pay back the IMF loans in 1984, it, however, again started borrowing from IMF, World Bank, and other commercial sources from 1985, to support the above mentioned subsidized sectors and for military purposes. When Rajiv Gandhi became the Prime Minister of India in 1984, after his mother Indira Gandhi was assassinated, he decided to break the path of socialist system of government control and restrictions, chosen by Nehru, and continued by his mother. Western educated and exposed to western culture, Rajiv Gandhi made the first economic liberation in India in 1985, by way of exempting sixteen industries from the monopolies, and lifting restrictions on trade; and easing and abolishing licenses on manufacturing investments in consumer goods. Moreover, the move to cut personal taxes and the liberalization on Foreign Direct Investment (FDI) encouraged more FDI and joint ventures between local and foreign companies, resulting in the entry of Pepsi company in India, and expansion of companies such as Suzuki in different states of India. This resulted in bringing more capital to the country on the one hand (Vietor 2007: 91), and on the other, freeing FDI from the tag of a taboo and making it indispensable for the development of the country. This move along with further liberalization by Rajiv Gandhi, was supported by the business community and a sizable section of academia, which included Manmohan Singh, who was the deputy chairman of planning commission, and later on Rajiv's economic advisor, and other western educated economists, besides external economic advisors from the World Bank and IFM. But on the other hand there was opposition to this move from a formidable section of the civil society, academia, and political parties such as BJP and Communist party, who saw this as a move towards going away from the path of self-sufficiency. Inside Rajiv's party—Congress—this move to further liberalization was also strongly contested by inside groups, who felt it will dent the socialist image of the party, and therefore may cause electoral loss (Manor 1987).

Rajiv's move of liberalization and opening up did bring some growth, nonetheless, India was still facing debt and oil crisis. This was happening in the midst of the fall of Soviet Union, of which India was an ally and was banking upon. In 1989 Rajiv Gandhi's assassination led to a political crisis in the Congress party on the one hand, and on the other hand, affected the already beleaguered economy. From 1989 to 1991 two governments changed, first came the National Front government, which accepted the structural adjustment program of IMF to get the loan; and then the Janata Dal which came to power in January 1991. But despite the changes in the government, India was still forced to take loans from IMF. The situation was turning out of hands, as India's foreign exchange reserves were, by now, just $1.2 billon (Ahluwalia 1994: 17). The only option left was to again seek IMF's assistance, but IMF's assistance does come with the conditions, which India's new government headed by Narsimha Rao, and more importantly its finance minister Manmohan Singh, were quite aware of. With this, India chose to airlift 25 tons of gold to the bank of England as a collateral for emergency loan, in case the agreement is not reached between IMF and Indian government (Vietor 2007).

Economic Reforms and Stress on Land

With Narsimha Rao taking over as the Prime Minister of India in July 1991, around 49 per cent of the industrial outputs were directly under the control of government and the banking and financial sector like insurance were hundred per cent controlled by the government. Rao, as mentioned in the previous section, chose Manmohan Singh as his finance minister. Interestingly, Manmohan Singh was not a Congress party member; therefore Rao brought an outsider to the party, and inducted him into the cabinet and gave him the crucial portfolio. It was not Rao's affiliation with Singh which made him take this decision, rather, it was Singh's reputation as an efficient Cambridge and Oxford trained development economist, which impressed Rao to choose Singh for the crucial job. Singh had served as the Governor of the Reserve Bank of India (RBI), Economic Advisor to National Front government, and had worked as Secretary General of the South Commission in Geneva, which had given him a good reputation among the business circles in India. He had also enjoyed a good equation with the higher echelons in IMF and World Bank as a pro-market economist (Vandana 2008). All these factors made Rao to include Singh in the cabinet to create momentum in Indian economy and bring what economists would say 'investor confidence'. Singh had all the ingredients to fulfil the crucial job. And to get his job done, he appointed his ilk Montek Singh Ahuluwalia, again a western trained pro-market economist, as his financial secretary, the job which Singh himself had done couple of years ago.

With Rao in command along with Manmohan Singh as Finance Minister, and Harvard trained P. Chidambaram as Commerce Minister, India moved towards structural adjustment programs, the programs which were required to get the IMF or World Bank loans, or commonly known as abiding or following the Washington consensus.[2] The government went ahead with following IMF conditions, partly though, therefore slashing subsidies, increasing interest rates to attract investor to government debt, devalued rupee, simplified procedures for FDI, which included lifting sealing on foreign investment to 51 per cent, and importantly, allowing public sector companies to forge partnership with private companies (Vietor 2007). In this way government took loans from IMF and the World Bank. While it was visibly seen as a triumph for Washington Consensus supporters over their opponents hailing from the Soviet Union block, however, in actual terms, in the Indian context it was India's domestic crisis and absence of the third option which made India to seek the help of Bretton

---

[2] Washington Consensus, a term coined by John Williamson, it refers to the ten policies which are associated with structural-adjustment loan from the IMF: These conditions are: fiscal discipline, tax reform, interest rate liberalization, a competitive exchange rate, removal of barriers to trade and barriers to foreign investment, privatization, deregulation, secure property rights, and increased public expenditure on health and education. See John Williamson (1990), 'What Washington means by Policy Reform' in *Latin American Adjustment: How Much Has Happened?* Washington DC: Institute for International Economics.

Woods institutions—rather than any love for them. This, however, does not mean there were no admirers for western led pro-market economy. There were, as mentioned above, names like Manmohan Singh, Ahluwalia, and scores of other technocrats, who were employed by Singh, Ahluwalia, and Chidambaram to make liberalization possible. Under these circumstances the zeal and encouragement for private investment led to the acquisition of lands in the country at a large pace. However, land acquisitions at this time could not create a wider debate among the intellectuals and in the media. And this was possibly the reason why the business class and rising new middle class was seeing these acquisitions and spread of industry as a window of economic development for the country. Moreover, liberalization during this phase took place in a phased manner. While the reforms, or commonly known 'hard reforms', which would hit the public directly, like subsidies on power sector, privatization of public sector, exit policy, and so on, were done in a phased manner and by checking public mood, the soft reforms on the other hand were done immediately to gain the confidence of IMF and other financial institutions.

The second phase of liberalization took place not during the Congress rule, but interestingly under the rule of BJP—the party which when in opposition, was opposing India's every move of liberalization. BJP came into power in 1998, after National Front government—the coalition of different parties—came together to form the government after the end of Rao's government in 1996. Since Congress could not get the number of seats required to form the government itself, it offered support to the National Front government to restrain BJP from forming the government. However, with the differences among coalition partners the National Front government could not last long, and elections were held in 1998, in which BJP came into power. It is here where BJP strategically drifted from its Swadeshi policy and initiated the second wave of liberalization in the form of phasing out restrictions on imports and moving towards integrating Indian economy with the global economy (Vandana 2008). BJP continued the policy of liberalization, even though it did not give up its core ideology of protecting national companies over 'western' companies. Interestingly, in the year 2000, BJP announced Special Economic Zone (SEZ) policy, to develop SEZs in a pattern similar to that of China, to get FDI in order to generate economic growth, and for infrastructure development. However, as the deliberations were going on in 2004, BJP lost the elections and Congress came to power at the Centre.

With Congress coming back to power, it chose Manmohan Singh as the Prime Minister of India and P. Chidambaram as the Finance Minister. Both Singh and Chidambaram, as mentioned above, were the architects of 1991 economic reforms and both coming back, with Ahluwalia, the old comrade of Singh, taking charge as the Deputy Chairman of the Planning Commission, of which Prime Minister is the chairman, new reforms were expected to take place. That is what happened in May 2005; the Indian parliament with not much noisy debate, which it is known for, passed the SEZ Act. Thus it ushered in the third wave of liberalization, the phase which shaped and sharpened public discourse and debate about land. The objectives of the SEZs are: (*a*) generation of additional economic activity, (*b*) promotion of exports of goods and services, (*c*) promotion of investment from domestic and foreign sources, (*d*) creation of employment opportunities, and (*e*) development of infrastructure facilities.[3]

Even though the passing of the Act did not catch much media attention nor was it debated thoroughly in public in initial days (Jonathan 2009), however, what followed was a rat-race among the states for investment. Interestingly, within two years since the Act was passed by the Indian Parliament, Government of India approved approximately 400 SEZs (Jonathan 2009). In this process of establishing SEZs, many states started taking a lead in putting up an investor friendly face, ignoring the concerns of peasants.

No doubt peasants started facing the wrath of capital in post-liberalization period, however, their concerns did not matter in pre-liberalization era either. Huge chunks of populations, especially the

---

[3] Information available on Ministry of Commerce and Industry website. See http://sezindia.nic.in/about-introduction.asp.

Adivasis (indigenous people) were displaced and dispossessed due to land acquisition for the 'national development projects'—steel plants, dams, and industrial areas—until the late 1980s; for which large swaths of land were acquired in the rural areas. For example, for Bhilai Steel Plant, in Chhattisgarh, land was acquired from 96 villages, spread over 15 kilometres (Parry 1999; Parry and Struempell 2008). The process of land acquisition, the impacts of acquisition, and compensation to the land has remained questionable. Most of the dispossessed and displaced people who had customary rights over land were not often given fair compensation or in certain cases no compensation at all; and promises of providing jobs were not kept either. This was true for Rourkela Steel Plant in Odisha, and for Durgapur Steel Plant in West Bengal as well (Parasuraman 1999; Parry and Struempell 2008). However, early 1970s marked the beginning of vocal opposition against the impacts of state led development projects on people and environment (Guha 2006). These social movements, including Naxalism, intensified after 1984 when amendments were brought into the 1894 Land Acquisition Act. These amendments allowed acquisition of land for any infrastructural development projects under the guise of public purpose. The dispossessed and displaced people offered resistance, albeit without any positive results (Guha 2008; Parry and Struempell 2008). It is estimated that over 60 million people, mostly scheduled castes and Adivasis got displaced between 1948 and 2008 due to these 'development' projects (Mathur 2008; Neef and Singer 2015). This process got intensified in post-liberalization period due to the construction of mega-dams for electricity generation, SEZs, and mining projects (Maitra 2009). With the penetration of capital in the resource rich regions, people's lands have been grabbed through extra-economic force, thereby snatching from them whatever little land they had in possession, especially in central India (Roy 2012).

While land acquisitions in pre-liberalization era were seemingly 'unexploitative' due to wider consensus for state led development, as a result pre-liberalization movement against steel plants, dams, and others, did not become successful. On the contrary, post-liberalization movement against the land-grabs, have, in certain cases, become very effective, a case in example, is Singur resistance against Tata projects or Nandigram resistance against the SEZs (Levien 2013).

These protests in West Bengal, Goa, Uttar Pradesh, and other areas have led to serious debates in India, therefore the Indian Parliament was forced to pass the new land Act, which would clearly define the public purpose and not allow the State to take land for the private sector. Therefore the Indian Parliament passed the Land Acquisition and Rehabilitation Act in September 2013, which allowed acquisition of agriculture land only if 80 per cent of the farmers will give their consent. The Act further stresses that multi-crop land should not be taken, because it affects the food security of the country. Nonetheless, the Act allows the land to be taken by the state for infrastructural development projects, such as HEPs, roads and railways, public institutions, and defence purposes, leaving enough space for the forcible acquisition of the land.

In the following section, I shall introduce Kashmir as a case *sui generis*, in the Indian constitution, and why land-grabs in Kashmir did not become a debate among scholars or media, unlike the land-grabs taking place in the rest of India. And more importantly, why new acquisition law will not prevent land-grabs in Kashmir.

Kashmir, a Case *Sui Generis* in Indian Constitution

Land-grabs in Kashmir can only be understood in light of the historical dimensions of the Kashmir conflict, which began with the partition of the Indian sub-continent in 1947 into the nation states of India and Pakistan. It is pertinent to mention that the partition plan of the British was based on the Two Nation Theory enacted through the Indian Independence Act, which provided options to the 562 princely states to either join India or Pakistan or remain independent. The decision had to be made by the ruler of the princely states keeping in mind the religious, cultural, and geographical considerations.

The princely state of Jammu and Kashmir located on the northern periphery of south Asia, surrounded (today) by Pakistan, China, and Afghanistan (see Map 3.2) did not join either India or Pakistan and

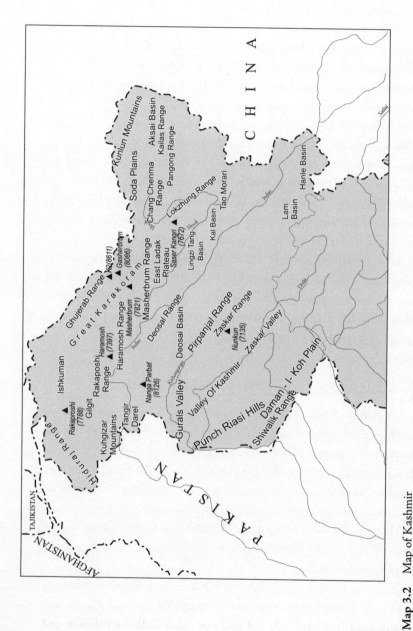

Map 3.2 Map of Kashmir

Source: Based on resources from University of Texas Libraries, University of Texas at Austin, September 2006.

Note: This map is not to scale and does not depict authentic political boundaries.

preferred to remain independent after August 1947, when the British paramountcy lapsed (Noronha 2007).

For three months, Kashmir remained independent, although not recognized by any international body. However, due to the revolt by the people of Poonch, against the excesses of the Maharaja to become a part of Pakistan, due to their religious, cultural, and geographical proximity with it (Rasool 2013), followed by the Pakistan backed tribal attack on 22 October 1947, from the north-western part of Pakistan to bring Kashmir into the Pakistani domain, the Maharaja of Kashmir sought military support from India to defend the area. India agreed to provide military support only if the Maharaja signed the instrument of accession with India. Ultimately on 26 October 1947, the instrument of accession was signed with the Indian union, and the Indian military landed in Kashmir to repel the tribal 'raiders'. The accession of Kashmir to the Indian state, however, was conditional, limited, and clearly stated that once law and order was restored and the invaders expelled, Kashmir's political status was to be determined as per the wishes of its people (Bose 2003). Pakistan however challenged the validity of the accession, which resulted in a brief war with India. The case was taken by India to the United Nations Security Council, which resulted in a ceasefire and subsequent division of Kashmir—with one part of Kashmir as *Azad* (independent) Kashmir, falling under Pakistani control, known as 'Pakistani administered Kashmir', and another part administered by India (Noronha 2007).

To maintain control over Kashmir, India used a two-pronged strategy: to gain political legitimacy, it started an election process. The 'elected' leaders would remain in power as long as they did not question the accession of Kashmir into India (Ganguly 1996). The Indian state used the client regimes in Kashmir to dilute the autonomy of Kashmir, which had been guaranteed to the region by Article 370 of the Indian Constitution. A plethora of legislations were passed by these sham Legislative Assemblies of Jammu Kashmir State government, which enabled the Indian Union government to strengthen it control over the political affairs of Kashmir state. To tighten its territorial control, India continued installation of military bases in Kashmir. The bases were first established in the mountains, far from residential areas. But later, bases were established in and around populated areas. A Kashmir based historian recollects how land was taken by the military in the early phase:

> Initially, they occupied important places such as airports and other places of security importance. During this time more land was taken by the Military, as the 1965 War between India and Pakistan occurred during this phase. However during and after 1971, the military occupied land adjacent to *Damdiner* Hills, which dominate the *Damdiner* valley. (Author interview with a university historian, June 2012)

As the stalemate over Kashmir continued, India and Pakistan fought three wars over it. These wars—in 1947, 1965, and 1999—brought more and more cantonments of military to Kashmir. Besides these, the 1961 war between India and China, and 1971 war between India and Pakistan over East Pakistan, which led to the creation of Bangladesh, further added to military escalation. In 1987, elections were held in Kashmir, which were won by the pro-independence party—Muslim United Front (MUF)—in some parts. However, the election officer under the influence of Indian state and the ruling party, National Conference, declared the results in favour of the National Conference candidate. Furthermore, MUF political activists and polling agents were imprisoned and tortured in custody which resulted in a shift in the MUF activists' political thinking; wherein it was believed that the scope for constitutional means of struggle did not exist in Kashmir. The tortured activists like Ajaz Dar, Ashfaq Majid, and Yasin Malik after their release from prisons, started the armed struggle in Kashmir as the foremost guerrilla commanders of the Jammu and Kashmir Liberation Front (JKLF), with the aim of forming an independent and sovereign Kashmir (Bose 2003). Here, what we see is the relative failure on the part of the state, to maintain a minimum level of political legitimacy. This is reflected in a rising insurgency problem, which then appears to threaten the territorial integrity of the region from the point of view of the Indian state.

Taking a pause from Kashmir's recent political history, a brief account of the development projects in the region, is important to take note of.

On the one hand, since 1947, the Government of India, as a strategic move, provided subsidizes on water, electricity, food, kerosene oil, health-care, and other daily necessities of life to win the 'hearts and minds' of people and to maintain political legitimacy in the region. On the other hand, Kashmir fitted into the Government of India's move or Nehruvian development model of constructing dams and power projects, whereby Kashmir's glacier-fed waters were seen as apt for cheap hydroelectricity generation, about which we shall discuss in detail in the next chapter. Thus HEPs construction was envisaged as part of state led development plan. However, contrary to the debate arising on the projects among the academic circles in India, in Kashmir, these HEPs did not become a matter of public discourse, nor did the impact of these HEPs on peasantry create any major resentment. The reasons being, (*a*) these projects being constructed in mountainous areas, where people's voices are not heard by the government authorities or media, and (*b*) these HEPs were projects as solving the electricity vows of the region.

As 1990s marked the beginning of insurgency, all economics related, resources related, and environment related issues took a back seat, and it was the fight for independence which was seen as the primary goal, and fighting against the construction of HEPs was seen as a secondary issue. This was also the phase where life and liberty was considered more precious, as getting killed at the hands of military or militants was quite common, and people would not venture out of their homes after 7 p.m. even during summer days. As militancy declined, the debate about HEPs started taking steam. However, the debate is still confined to the media only, whereby, the story about state's water exploitation makes the news, but not the effects of these projects on the peasantry. Likewise, academic scholarship has, by and large, neglected research on Kashmiri peasantry and agrarian struggles. However, lately, as the HEPs are being constructed, the debate has been taking place in local assembly, among the political parties, and at the civil society level about the fallout of these HEPs on the political economy of Kashmir.

To go back to the question of Kashmir's political history and its relation with the Indian state, any development in Kashmir would not be seen as a project run for the national development. Rather these projects/HEPs are seen as a part of imperialism, whereby, the outsider state takes the resources of the other state. Therefore, the state of India is seen here as the other. This perception about Indian state was reverberated by none else than a pro-India party leader and present Chief Minister of the state, Mehbooba Mufti in October 2013, when she was leader of the opposition in lower house of the Jammu and Kashmir assembly, she said: 'India is treating Kashmir like a colony'. These words were obviously a reflection of the common perception about India in Kashmir. Therefore, the HEP construction in Kashmir by the state-owned corporation—NHPC—is not only to be understood and explained here as an outside corporate working for power generation, but a corporation—almost on the similar lines of EIC—extracting the regions resources for the Centre.

***

The trajectory of India's development from the colonial period to the present times, as presented above gives us an idea how India has, so far, largely followed the colonial approach towards land appropriation. After independence, the Indian state followed a nationalistic path of development, however the developmental approach of the state was far from being pro-peasant and/or pro-ecology. India moved partly away from the nationalist Swadeshi development path in 1980, towards partial liberalization, and finally moved further away from Swadeshi mode of development to liberalization in 1990. And finally, in 2005 it took the step towards creating the SEZs which brought the debate about the land into focus. However, while all these phases took place; one thing among them was common—all of the phases of development, whether pre-independence phase in the form of railways construction or in the post-independence development projects, peasants and rural folk were neglected in the larger debate. It is only after SEZs were formed and the large chunks of land in urban areas like West Bengal or Noida were taken control of, and people dispossessed, that land became a topic of debate. Similar or graver atrocities in the name of development have been happening to the peasants in the countryside for decades, but they do not come into the limelight.

In a similar fashion, hydroelectricity projects in Kashmir which were developed by NHPC from the 1970s, have been displacing thousands of peasants from their lands and houses. However, they are yet to become a debate in the media, in the policy circles, or in academia in India. What is interesting is that these projects did not even become debatable in Kashmir either in the late 2000, as most of the literature on Kashmir, was/is focused on Kashmiris' political struggle. However, as relative normalcy returned to the valley, the construction of these HEPs have taken a debate and a mode of resistance in the region. We shall discuss the HEPs, actors, impacts, narratives, and resistance in the next two chapters.

4 From Land Tenure Changes to Land-Grabs

When we deal with the crucial topic of land, especially land tenure relations, and land-grabs and agrarian class structures, it becomes imperative to go back to the historical roots of landownership and property rights of the peasants. Ignoring the historical lenses of the land tenure relations would mean that the current land relations/landownership means were always like this. Digging deep, this chapter first traces the history of land rights in Kashmir and argues that landownership rights in Kashmir were introduced in the fifth century AD and they continued until the eighteenth century AD, whereas in rest of the Indian subcontinent land rights were introduced by British Raj, on the contrary, Kashmir enjoyed land rights up until 1846. As the British sold the region to the Dogra in 1846, Kashmir lost the ownership right of the land until the end of autocratic rule in 1947. Dogras treated Kashmir and its dependencies as their personal property and imposed cruel methods of taxation besides denying them the right to move or migrate. Prior to that, peasants were proud owners of the land, living on subsistence or what Scott (1976) calls, a 'unit of production and a unit of consumption'. Therefore, overall peasantry was in general an egalitarian system. However, the end of the Dogra rule led to the formation of new Kashmir, with people again having rights on land and property. Today, as we show in this chapter, the owners of land and property are now turning homeless due to land-grabs by the domestic capital. This is happening despite the presence of a 'democratic government'.

This chapter begins with the historical account of land rights and land tenure changes in Kashmir. It then moves on to explain how land reforms in Kashmir looked like and how they took place. It further discusses how the peasants' land rights were restored due to land reforms. It illustrates how land reforms helped in the income enhancement of some of the peasants, which created outward mobility of people through multiple livelihoods. However, it created a class division among the erstwhile egalitarian peasants.

The chapter further discusses the historical background of Badwan and Khopri in Gurez, besides presenting the geographical, administrative, and brief socio-economic sketch of the two villages. It moves on to narrate the process of land acquisition and the arrival of external capital in the area of Gurez. It stresses on how the land was taken arbitrarily by the State. Finally the chapter provides concluding remarks about the themes discussed in this chapter.

Land Tenure Changes, Landlordism, and Peasant Exploitation

Land tenure changes due to modern capital in the hilly areas of Kashmir, like Badwan and Khopri in Gurez, can only be explained historically by looking at land tenure changes, land rights, and landownership in Kashmir under different regimes. To begin with, we go back to the period (AD 515–1320) when Kashmir was under Hindu rulers. Kalhana (1979) gives us a thought provoking account of this period by stating that the landownership during this period lay with the individuals. Land transactions were done between the individuals and the deals were recorded in Registrar of Real Estate Sale deeds. The ruler would solve the disputes if they arose during the transactions (Stein 1979). However, it is not clear whether total ownership of the land was with the ruler during this time, as many cases of land being given to the officials in lieu of their services, scholar's religious places, and other public spaces were found (Kawa 2008). These lands which were granted to the people, made them wealthy and powerful, and gave them the title of *Damaras*, a formidable force, who because of their wealth and personal army, refused to pay taxes to the king. Thus, Damaras represented medieval century landlords or feudal lords.

These Damaras were, however, cut to size by the kings in the later stages, by taking their land back, which reflects that the total ownership of the land was with the king and the land given to Damaras was a form of grant and not ownership.

After the end of the Hindu period, began the Sultanate or Muslim period (1320–1586). Here what becomes clear is that individuals still held the private land and could sell or buy it, but were paying taxes to the king. However, at the same time, the state-owned the major part of the land, called *Khalsa* (state land) in many villages wherefrom it would get the revenue. Here the practice of granting the land to the people with proximity to the leader, religious institutions etc. continued. But, unlike the Hindu period, the state could not take the land back once it was given to an individual or an institution (Kawa 2008).

The end of the Sultanate period in 1586 marked the beginning of the Mughal (1586–1753) and Afghan (1753–1819) periods. This is the time when Kashmir lost its sovereignty to the external rulers—the Mughals. While Hindus and Sultans were local rulers, Mughals invaded Kashmir and brought it under their control. Nonetheless, they did not snatch the property rights of the peasants. The latter still used to own the arable and non-arable land against which they, however, had to pay taxes to the rulers (Habib 2013). Besides these lands, people would collectively exercise their rights on *Kahcharai* (grazing land) in villages to graze their cattle. One interesting fact was that the regime would never dislodge the owners from their lands. This does not mean that Mughal or Afghan rule was benevolent. It was occupational, draconian and exploitative in nature.

However, it is important to mention here that by dint of having ownership right, the right to sell, control and grant the land and to employ
labour on it, made the peasants not only *de facto* but also *de jure* owners
of the land. However, that did not solve their problems. Peasants had to
pay 75 per cent of their produce as a tax to the State, which would many
times lead them to starvation and if they were lucky enough, just enough
to feed themselves. Under those circumstances, what is observed is that
the peasants tried to alienate themselves from their land by selling it off.
But it was not often possible to sell the land due to the abundance of
land available, the limited purchasing power of the people, the absence of
labour force and the absence of agricultural technology to cultivate land
(Kawa 2008).

The end of Afghan Period in AD 1819 marked the brief spell of 27
years of Sikh rule (1819–46). Not much change was observed during this
time in terms of peasant ownership of land. Peasants continued owning
personal property; and now it was also legalized. Any transaction of the
land was to be formalized by paying 2.5 anna of court fee. Like their
predecessors, Sikh rulers also extracted their revenue from agriculture by
levying taxes on the peasantry.

The Sikhs were replaced by the Dogras in 1846, and their rule lasted till
1947. Whereas Kashmir lost its sovereignty in 1586 itself to Mughals, the
region and its dependencies got enslaved with the arrival of the Dogra rule
which came into existence through the Treaty of Amritsar. This Treaty
was signed between the English EIC and Maharaja Gulab Singh, the first
Dogra ruler of Kashmir, on 16 March 1846 (Rai 2004). Under the Treaty,
the EIC transferred the region of Kashmir to the Maharaja for 75 lakh
Nanak Shahi rupees (Puri 1981).[1] With the Dogras taking over Kashmir,

---

[1] Article 1 of the Treaty states,

[T]he British government transfers and makes over forever, in independent
possession, to Maharaja Gulab Singh and his heirs male of his body, all the hilly or
mountainous country with its dependencies situated to the east ward of the river
Indus and Westward of the river Ravi, including Chamba and excluding Lahol, being
part of the territories ceded to the British Government by the Lahore state according
to the provisions of Article IV of the treaty of Lahore dated 9th March, AD 1846.

they declared private ownership of property land as null and void, and brought all the land under State control (Aziz 2010). This resulted in peasantry losing the ownership of land, which they were owning from centuries. With the Maharaja taking control of the land, he transferred huge chunks of land called Jagirs (assigned tracts of land) to a neo-class of intermediaries to create a support base. These intermediaries, mostly Hindus, were different types of landlords with varied designations, called Jagirdars (assignees), Muafidars, Illaqadars and Chakdars (land holders exempt from payment of revenue), and Pattadars (rent receiver of a piece of land) and were actually collaborators of feudal Lord Maharaja (Beg 1995). Even though the Jagir was not a permanent transfer of ownership of land to the Jagirdar, yet they acted as masters and used cruelty against the tenants (Aziz 2010). Under those circumstances, peasants turned from owners of land to mere 'serfs', as they did not have even right to cultivation or right to occupancy of land, rather they were tied to it, not even allowed to move out, instead were forced to cultivate the land (Beg 1995: 36; Lawrence 2002: 2–3). However, despite restrictions imposed on migration, many of the peasants managed to 'flee' to Punjab and other regions to escape the rant of landlords and the Raj. In short, peasantry in this period not only lost the ownership but also had to face immense miseries at the hands of intermediaries and the State which appropriated major portion of their produce, leaving just a meagre amount for their survival. Moreover, the State also levied huge taxes, which put further burden on the already beleaguered peasantry. The realm of British India's Non-Interventionist Policy in the region, which was due to the fact that they had sold the region to the Dogras, changed with the appointment of British Resident in 1885 in Kashmir to work for the reforms in the Dogra state. This appointment was made after the grievances were made to the British crown against the Dogra rule which had crossed the limits of cruelty (Aziz 2010). The exploitation of Indian resources and the very imposition of inhuman laws on peasantry by British in India are well established, however in Kashmir the very intervention of British crown in the state was seen as a blessing, as the Dogra rule in Kashmir was more exploitive and cruel than the British rule in the rest of India (Aziz 2010).

With the appointment of a Resident, which coincided with the Maharaja Pratap Singh taking reigns of the region from (1885–1925), the settlement and restoration of the property rights was felt necessary to maintain control on the region. Nonetheless, the appointment of the first Settlement Officer Mr Wingate did not serve the purpose until the new settlement officer Mr Lawrence took the charge as the Permanent Settlement officer. Although, before leaving the office, Mr Wingate had raised the issue of abuses done to the people in Kashmir and suggested measures to fix them (Lawrence 2002: 424). The appointment of Lawrence led to the restoration of peasants rights and paved the way for land settlement. While Lawrence is still highly regarded in Kashmir, nevertheless, in his own account, he appreciated the support he was provided by the Dogra regime. This was, to believe, that he never wanted to change the larger structure of the system, but wanted to give rights to the peasants, but these rights were also half-baked as the peasants would cultivate the land but the larger benefits would be yielded by the landlords (Aziz 2010; Kawa 2008; Lawrence 2002).

Though with Lawrence led settlement, the condition of the peasants improved to a certain extent, but in general, the miseries of peasants continued, resulting in a peasant revolt against the Dogra rule in 1931. The 1931 uprising, as well as the pressure from the British Resident mounted on the Maharaja to constitute a Committee to look into the problems faced by the Muslims. In this regard, a Commission under B.J. Glancy was appointed on 12 November 1931. The Commission advocated the representation of Muslims in service, and ownership rights of the peasants on land, but again, without really affecting the *Jagirdari* or Landlordism. In the meantime, Muslim Conference, which was now a newly formed political party, represented the aspirations of the peasants. In his presidential addresses to All Jammu and Kashmir Muslim Conference on 15–17 October 1932, 15–17 December 1933, and March 1938, Sheikh Mohammad Abdullah, who had then emerged as the tallest leader against the Maharaja's autocratic rule, demanded ownership rights of the peasantry. Like Sheikh, other leaders of the Muslim Conference were also fighting for peasants' cause (Kawa 2008: 228). This demand became louder when the Muslim Conference split into two groups and Sheikh Abdullah formed Jammu and Kashmir National Conference, as a secular party, in the year 1939. The party draws its support from peasants and also galvanizes them to fight for their rights. In this context the party came up with a manifesto called *Naya Kashmir* (New Kashmir) on 30 March 1944, which carried an overall plan for the socio-economic development of the state. Importantly, Article 50 of the manifesto is devoted to the 'Peasant Charter' that described how the party would bring peasants out of landlordism, debt crisis, and would empower them after the end of the autocratic rule. As 1947 marked the end of the Dogra rule, and National Conference formed the interim government, it took on the mission of land reforms.

Land Reforms: From the Abolition of Landlordism to the (Re)Establishment of Agrarian Class

With the end of Dogra despotic rule, Sheikh took over reigns of Kashmir. After assuming power in 1948, Sheikh worked on modalities of land reforms, which he had promised to the masses. On 13 July 1950, Sheikh fulfilled his promise to the people and announced some of the most sweeping land reforms:

> ... any person or institute within the territories of Jammu and Kashmir State, possessing more than one thousand kanals (50 hectares) of land in proprietary, shall forfeit all such lands, except 160 kanals (eight hectares) of agricultural land for his personal maintenance, in favour of the tiller thereof subject to the rules and regulations, in force as regards collection of land revenue etc. with effect from today, only the tillers of these lands will be recognized as the proprietors, who will be sole owners of the next kharif crop.[2]

These land reforms that took place in the three phases: 1948–53, 1954–74, and 1975 (Beg 1995: II–III), have achieved their primary

---

[2] Government of Jammu and Kashmir, Abolition of Big landlordism: Text of announcement, 13 July 1950 at Lal Chowk, Srinagar, The Press Information Bureau.

goal of abolition of landlordism, giving land to the tiller, ceiling on land-holdings, and abolition of intermediaries. While incomes of peasants increased, with the peasantry engaging in multiple livelihoods it created further class divisions, albeit competitive against coercive divisions, among the peasantry. In this regard, the first step that was taken was, that all the Jagirs were abolished, except in the case of those given to religious institutions. Some of the other major highlights of the reforms were:

1. Abolition of Jagirs, *Muafis*, and *Mukararies*.[3]
2. Elimination of all rights, titles, and interests of hitherto intermediaries or ex-proprietors; and their instant transfer to the actual tillers, free of any price or compensation.
3. Grant of ownership restricted to 182 kanals or 23 acres including trees, wells, tanks, ponds, water channels, and land pathways.
4. Declaration of land rights of peasants as lawful and permanent conditioning constant cultivation.
5. Retrieval of grass farms, fuel reserves, and common land for distribution among the landless and others in proportion to their landholdings.
6. Right to inheritance on landed property and condoning of long-pending peasants debts.

With these land reforms 'from above'[4] taking place in Kashmir, along-side the modernizing regimes of the Shah of Iran, Nehru in India, and Nasser in Egypt (Bernstein 2010), the abolition of Big Lands Estates Act 1948 led to 55 lakh kanals of land being transferred to the tillers, which enabled them to earn the yield based on the labour they put in (Kawa 2008: 231). This not only helped the peasants to overcome their economic depri-vation but also gave them ownership rights of the land, which ultimately elevated their social status. While majority of the peasants benefitted from these land reforms, in case of a portion of the people of the Shia sect of

---

[3] The Muafis were grants in shape of charity to individuals, institutions, and such other bodies. The Mukararies were the cash grants given to an individual, institutions, and saintly persons (Aziz 2010).

[4] Land reforms initiated by the governments.

Muslims,[5] land reforms did not bring about much benefit. Rather they had a negative impact on the social status of those who received land during the land reforms. This was due to the fatwa (decree) issued by one of the most respected Shia religious leaders, Agha Syed Yousuf, against land reforms, terming them as 'un-Islamic', because he believed that only the landowners, who were in this case erstwhile landlords, had the right on their land and snatching their 'right' would be 'un-Islamic' and those who took the land would be declared as *gassibs* (grabbers). Local people believed that Shia religious leaders were beneficiaries of landlordism, therefore issuing fatwa against land reforms was aimed to serve their personal interests. This fatwa largely prevailed among the major section of Shia community over the political sanctity of land reforms, thereby preventing them from taking lands; nevertheless many from the Shia community quietly took the land. The people who took the land are still treated as gassibs, as they disrespected the decree.[6] This not only challenged the notion that land reforms benefited all but it also questioned the Sheikh's 'autonomy and capacity' to implement them. There is no doubt that the Sheikh and his government provided peasants legal sanctions to own the land, however, Shia religious cleric's fatwa challenged the State's authority, and is therefore quite a reflection of Fox's (1993) analytical approach 'Autonomy and capacity': the two dimensions of state power to function. Fox sees power as a matter of degrees that can shift and change over time, however slightly or temporarily, with different combinations of degrees of autonomy and capacity depending on the issue relative to other factors and actors. Here what is observed is that, while Sheikh had an autonomy and capacity to lead land reforms, yet due to the Shia religious leader's influence, a sizable chunk of population did not benefit from them.

Nevertheless, unlike many other places in the world, land reforms in Kashmir ran smoothly without the need of extreme force. This was made possible by the fact that Sheikh and his party awakened Kashmiri

---

[5] Kashmir has 97 per cent Muslim population. Majority of the people follow Sunni sect of Islam and the minority follow Shia sect of Islam.

[6] Author interview with local Shia Scholar from Srinagar, December 2013.

peasantry to fight against the despotic Dogra system, and brought Kashmir out of Dogra rule, which gave him legitimacy to lead and decide on behalf of the peasants. This was further possible because of the fact that the state continued to allow landlords having land up to five acres, provided they cultivate it and live in their native villages. Moreover, they were obliged to pay the taxes to the State in accordance with the law (Beg 1995). These erstwhile landlords were now just as peasants themselves, as they had lost the powers and control on peasantry, much like in other Indian states where landlordism is now a concept of the past (Harriss 2013).

The land reforms in Kashmir henceforth provided an opportunity to the peasants to cultivate their own land. Moreover, the government initiated a series of agricultural and developmental policies for the improvement of the people. This was important for a region that had just come out of the authoritarian rule (Aziz 2010), which can be stated from the fact that 'in 1950, the state had a meagre per-capita income of 208 rupees (at 1960–1 prices) and the rate of literacy was just about 5 per cent, while Indian literacy rate was 18.33 per cent' (Aziz 2010: 7). Therefore it was necessary for the government to push for the development of agriculture and allied sectors—the main livelihoods of people. Within this realm, the ownership of land together with the support of the government, enabled people to slowly embark on the development path. As people could produce enough food to feed themselves, besides grazing cattle and sheep, and sending their wards to schools, this helped in the upward social mobility of the peasants (Kawa 2008). This increase in economic production, however, led to the migration of people from hilly areas such as Gurez to the valley—for better education and better living.

Badwan and Khopri

Badwan, and Khopri, the two villages fall in the picturesque Gurez valley of the administrative district of Bandipora, around 140 kilometres from Srinagar, the summer capital of Kashmir. Tehsil Gurez, as per the 2011 census, has a population of 37,000, consisting 28 villages, at about 8,000 feet above the sea level, and is situated within 34° 25′ North latitude and 74° 38′ East longitude, with lush green meadows, pine forests, and the trout-filled Kishanganga river which comes through these rich meadows, falls on the old Silk Road, which prior to 1947 connected Kashmir to Central Asia and China through Gilgit–Baltistan in Pakistan. Gurez valley is inhabited by tribal people, known as Dard-Sheena. Prior to 1948, it was a part of Gilgit–Baltistan region (now part of Pakistan). However after the 1948 settlement, Gurez became part of Indian administered Kashmir. Geographically, the land got divided between India and Pakistan (even though still disputed) along with 80 per cent of the population that shared the same culture, language, and traditions. The majority of Dard-Sheena population now lives in Gilgit, Pakistan; the minority, 20 per cent, is living in the Indian side of Kashmir, in Gurez. Like many other people of various small valleys in Kashmir, such as Karnah valley, Bangus valley, Lolab valley, and so on; people of Gurez valley are in actual terms hilly people or what are known as 'Zomies', even though the existing literature on Zomies, including Scott (2010), has not made reference of Kashmir zomie areas.

Located on the zero point Line of Control (LoC) of divided Kashmir on Indian side, Gurez is completely landlocked, with only one motorable road, which remains closed for more than six months during winters due to heavy snowfall. Being on the zero point LoC, Gurezees have not actively participated in armed movements due to the landlocked nature of the territory and military fortification. Gurez is also described as most peaceful area in terms of zero per cent crime rate recorded by the local police here. However, Gurezees, like citizens of other highly 'disturbed' areas near the LoC, must possess a special border pass issued by the District Magistrate to enter or leave from Gurez. They are considered as 'sympathizers of Kashmir freedom movement' who give shelter to the infiltrators from Pakistan. Thus the 'special' entry and exit pass is as important for them as a passport to travel to any other country. Likewise, outside visitors need to get a travel permission card, issued by the District Police Commissioner—Application for Travel.

A permit is like applying for a visa. Identity card, in case of foreigner's passport, two photographs along with application letter explaining the travel dates, and purpose of visit has to be submitted to Superintendent of Police's office at Bandipora, who will issue the permit card within three working days, unless there is no adverse security report of the applicant. This card has to be shown at various check points while entering or exiting the Gurez valley.

Gurez has two administrative blocks—Daver and Tulail—both often in confrontation on political and economic fronts. One shows supremacy over the other. Out of 28 villages in Gurez, 15 are in Tulail, giving it an edge over main Gurez valley; but the Daver block consisting of 13 villages, has always enjoyed political, economic, and administrative supremacy due to its location, the human resources it has produced, and the political control it exercises. Major characteristics of Gurez are given in Table 4.1. At Daver, the central place in Gurez, is located the Tehsildar's (land records/administrator's) office, police station, health clinic, Sub-Judicial Magistrate's Office, Fire and Emergency Services Station, Higher Secondary School, Tourist Reception Centre, and a small market. Daver is, thus, centre of all activities for the people of Gurez, as well as for the people of Badwan and Khopri, which are 5 kilometres and 7 kilometres away from Daver, respectively. Whether it is for the students to go to school, or to buy daily or weekly stock of food, or to notarize land transactions, get police verification, see a doctor, and so on, people often have to ferry to district headquarter Bandipora to get their administrative issues addressed and for various other items of necessity, which are not available in the Daver market.

The administrative district Bandipora was carved out of the administrative district of Baramulla in 2007 and became the 14th district in the state in terms of its population size of 3,06,881 persons on a geographical area of 398 sq. kilometres (Census 2011). Bandipora is surrounded by the administrative districts of Baramulla, Kupwara, Ganderbal, and Srinagar. Here in Bandipora you have the District Commissioner's Office, District Superintendent of Police's Office, District and Sessions Judge's Court, District Chief Education Officer's Office, and other administrative heads offices, besides many banks and colleges. Getting to Bandipora takes people of the Gurez valley an entire day. With no frequent transport available, high-engine vehicles ferry passengers and charge each of them 600 rupees (USD 12) for a roundtrip, which is roughly equal to the amount of money for which a five-member family can feed itself for a week. The mountainous

Table 4.1 Major Characterizes of Gurez

Major Characteristics			Area and Population		
S. No	Particulars	Profile	S. No	Particulars	No.
1.	Geographical distribution	−28 villages −10 panchayats, −2 blocks (Dawer and Tulail), −one Tehsil/Assembly consitituncy	1.	Area (sq. km)	362.88
2.	Principal crops/ fruits	Maize, wheat, pulses, millets, and vegetables	2.	Population (2001 census) Male and Female	28,786 15,309 13,477
3.	Major livestock	Sheep, goat, local cow, yak, horses, and mules	3.	Density of population (per sq. km)	79
4.	Average land holdings (ha)	0.278	4.	Literates to total population (%)	43
5.	Net irrigated area (%)	40	5.	Rural population as percentage to total population	Rural
6.	Soils	Sandy loam	6.	Schedule Tribe population (%)	100
7.	Major river	Kishenganga	7.	Below Poverty Line population	8,750
8.	Altitude range (m amsl)	2,460–39,000	8.	AAY population	6,590
9.	Average annual rainfall (mm)	5–30	9.	Working force (100%)	10,075
10.	Temperature (°C)	Max. (25) Min. (−20)		(a) Cultivators (%)	45
11.	Thermal index	Very cold		(b) Agricultural labourers (%)	10
12.	Hydric index	Humid		(c) Household industry (%)	20
				(d) Others (%)	35

Source: Shabir et al. (nd).

terrain, closure of roads for six months and the very absence of basic amenities of life even de-motivates government officials to work here. They also see it as a punishment posting for not succumbing to the pressures of higher authorities to do what they feel is unjust. However, the locals believe that only the 'inefficient' government officials, doctors, teachers, and others, who can not perform at the district headquarters are posted in Gurez. This, they believe, is the reason of abysmal governance there.

Travelling from Bandipora to Gurez, the 86 kilometres hilly rough terrain of zigzag bumpy roads, nevertheless, with beautiful scenery, which ideally should take one or two hours, takes minimum six to seven hours. After descending from a height of 11,672 feet, from *Razadan* top, and reaching a plane site, what one sees is the ongoing construction of a dam for KHEP. Heavy machinery in the forest area, the tunnels under construction, the deserted agriculture land—it is Badwan. Two roads leading to Badwan, one major semi-macadamized road and the other smaller link road, pass through the agricultural fields. The main road of Badwan is on the banks of river Kishanganga. This road connects Badwan with the main road of Gurez, which leads to Daver at the newly constructed police post—and the end of dam site. Just a few kilometres away from the newly constructed Police Station is Daver Bridge, which one has to cross to move towards the Khopri road.

Badwan, 'the big forest', village with 479 households, as per the 2011 census, has the distinction of being centrally located in Gurez valley, where every neighbouring villager would prefer to live in, and every elite would like to have a piece of land to use for business venture, a tourist hut or to build a house on the banks of Kishanganga river, facing the lush green forests. The location is a source of attraction for insiders as well as the travellers. A peasant finds it to be a fertile land, with availability of water for irrigation and to cultivate food, so does a businessman who finds the place suitable for opening a small business venture. Besides its prime location, the village enjoys supremacy among all the neighbouring villages of Gurez, as most of the top level government officers, teachers, and other technocrats of Gurez come from this village. Besides local government officers, some of the senior government bureaucrats and police officers also hail from this village, which include the local lawmaker and deputy speaker of the Jammu and Kashmir Assembly—Nazir Gurezi. Thus the village represents, on the one hand a group of elites who are not only influential at the local Tehsil level but also at the State level, and on the other hand, subsistent peasants—the majority of the village population—lives here.

Historically, the village came into existence due to inward migration of people from Bandipora, Pakistan, Afghanistan, and other places, as nomads, but later these people settled here, permanently.[7] But in the present times, the village is seeing an outward migration to Bandipora and Srinagar.

Located on the banks of Kishanganga on the back side, and facing the lush green forests on the front side, the traditional houses here are made of logs of woods. Every house is two storied; the first floor is used as a cow shed or to house buffalos and sheep, and the second floor consists of one or two bed rooms, kitchen, and bathroom (see Figure 4.1).

The toilets are made of wood, and are situated near the house. However, well-to-do families have decorated and well-furnished houses made of bricks or wood. There are some abandoned houses as well. These houses are of absentee landlords and some village elites, whose houses are registered here, but who actually live in Srinagar or Bandipora. In actual terms they have fully or partially migrated from here but on government records they are still the residents of this village.

Inside the village a small street connects all the households. The houses here are scattered, surrounded by agricultural fields, and fall either on the left or right side of the street. Here, in the middle of the road on the bridge, is a small shop of a young man Mushtaq, who sells potato chips, cigarettes, candles, and candies. There are two other small shops nearby Mushtaq's shop. One is near the *Haji's* (village elites) house; the other is near the village leader Azad's house. However, the prime location of Mushtaq's shop, makes it a place for foyer politics, where young and old sit to discuss local politics. Next to Mushtaq's shop is a Masjid (mosque). The Masjid does not only unite people for prayers, it also connects them

[7]   Interview with the peasants of Badwan, June 2012.

Figure 4.1 Houses in Badwan
Source: Shuaib Masoodi.

with other village mates. It is also the place where village leaders get to speak to others to take decisions about the welfare of the villages, discuss government led development, and healthcare and education schemes. If the government has to serve some notice or information for the peasants, they post it on the wall of the mosque (see Figure 4.2).

In winters, the mosque becomes the most happening place, as the road to Bandipora is closed, and discussions and gossips before and after the prayers inside the mosque are the favourite pastime of the people. While in the summers, the bank of the *throuth Kole* (trout stream), which flows outside the mosque, is a favourite place for people to sit and discuss the village politics, government issues, gossips, India and Pakistan relations, and of course, the crop yields and issues related to agriculture—main livelihood of the people.

Khopri (mountain) village, as per the 2011 census, has around 97 families residing there (see Figure 4.3). But in reality, not more than thirty households are present in this village—which falls not far from Badwan. Badwan and Khopri are separated by Kishanganga river. Seen from the

Figure 4.2 Government Notification for Compensation of Land, pasted on Masjid Wall in Badwan
Source: Author.

main road of Gurez, Kishanganga falls on the backside of Badwan, and flows on the front side of Khopri. The zigzag and sloppy seven kilometres narrow road from Dawer on the banks of Kishanganga, on India-Pakistan border, fenced with razor-sharp concertina wire on the right, leads to

Figure 4.3   Khopri Village
Source: Author.

Khopri and ends at the centre of the village, the location of local mosque. Figure 4.4 presents a view of the Dawar-Khopri road.

On the revenue records Khopri is named as Hastand Khopri, because earlier, the people of Khopri used to live in Hustand, a village next to Daver. As per local accounts the village is around just 60 years old. Prior to 1947, that is, before the Indian army came here to fight against the Pakistani 'intruders' and 'occupied' the land at Hastand, people used to graze cattle at Khopri Mountains and lived there during summers, moving back to Hastand in winters. When the military occupied the land at Hastand, people permanently moved their residence to Khopri. While majority of people moved to Khopri post military occupation of Hastand, people of the Mir clan—the biggest clan in the village—claim that they have been living in the village from over 100 years. They do not find the roots of the village as of 1947, but rather trace back the origin of this village to 90–100 years ago, that is, when their great-grandfather Mukhtar Mir moved his

Figure 4.4 The Road that Connects Khopri with Dawar, is Fenced with Razor-Sharp Concertina Wire from Pakistan's Side to Prevent Infiltration
Source: Author.

residence from Hastand to Khopri, to be nearer to the cow/sheep sheds to take care of livestock. This gave birth to a village, namely Khopri.[8] From one family of Mukhtar Mir, with his four sons, who after marriage separated into four families, the village saw some people from Pakistani side of Kashmir migrating here. This clan—Nasirs—now numbers 12 families in the village. Besides Mirs and Nasirs the village has two Lone families and one Dar family living here. In general, out of 30 households, the village is predominated by Mirs.

Khopri is a mirror image of mountainous villages in Kashmir. Here well-to-do families live mostly near the road, while the less privileged live away from it. For example, Akbar Mir—village head, who passed his high school in the 1970s—did not opt for a government job, the

[8] Since the village is located on the mountain, it is called Khopri.

norm for educated people here. He instead raised his sheep, cows, and horses, besides tilling his own 12 kanals of land, and is residing near the mosque on the main road. While Aziz Mir, and his son Altaf, live near the school, both of them work as casual labourers. The houses here are made of wood, very much alike the houses in Badwan or other parts of Gurez. Geographically, the village is hillier than Badwan. If the Indo-Pakistan border is a few yards away from Badwan, Khopri is located exactly on zero point of the LoC.

When the militancy started in the year 1989 in Kashmir, which was followed by cross-border firing between the two countries, many people from Khopri migrated to the nearby village Wanpora, as it would become the first target of cross-border firing from the Pakistan side. Inside the village, there are not many happening places, except Bashir and Ahmad's shops—the two small shops—which become meeting points for young and old, to buy cigarettes, potato chips, and candles. Quite akin to what has been observed in Badwan, these two shops, besides the mosque, represent places of discussion, leisure, gossips, and everyday politics. In Figure 4.5 author interviews a village leader outside the mosque. Here the villagers associate themselves with different political parties, while some others see themselves as neutral, however their political affiliation does not create any clash at the local level. The villagers live in peaceful coexistence, the reflection of which is that any villager can enter into his/her neighbour's house without permission or prior approval.

Both Badwan and Khopri have class differences, although in Khopri this difference is not as wide as we observe in Badwan. The class difference in Badwan is largely due to the educational, economic, and social inequalities that have arisen after well-to-do families began fully, or partially, migrating out of Gurez. While the partial/permanent migration of the people of Khopri—now about ten families—to Bandipora or Srinagar has been observed, but this migration is seen as necessary for the education of their wards—a common phenomenon in Gurez. Unlike Badwan, where the absentee landlords/elites (mostly government officers) have permanently moved to Srinagar or Bandipora, and seldom visit their native village; the relatively well-to-do families of Khopri,

Figure 4.5   Interview with the Village Leader
Source: Aijaz Mir.

who have houses in Bandipora or Srinagar, visit or mostly live, at least during summers, in Khopri.

Nevertheless, migration for education, or in certain cases for better life, has been happening for a long time in Badwan and Khopri. First was the Anwar Samoon's family who sent their kids to Bandipora and Srinagar to study. After completing their education, they qualified for Civil Service Exams and became government officers. This trend paved the way for many others who started migrating out for education and government jobs. This resulted, on the one hand, in more income coming to the villages; but on the other hand, it also created a class of people who became partial peasants, and later absentee landlords. According to the 2011 census data, Badwan and Khopri together consist of 576 households. If the figures are to be separated, it would be 479 households from Badwan and 97 households from Khopri. However, in reality, not more than 90 families in Badwan and 20 families in Khopri presently live there and the rest of them have already migrated (fully/partially) to Srinagar or Bandipora. The migrated families do not want to shun their village citizenship, because doing so, would lead to giving up their Scheduled Tribe status, which gives them reservations in government jobs and scholarships. While scholarships and government schemes are meant to serve those who live in the far-flung areas, in contrast here, the benefits are yielded by well-to-do families, who educate their kids in other cities; the poor remain at the margins.

With the influx of well-to-do people, from Gurez to the cities, which increased due to land reforms led income enhancement, yet a sizeable number of families chose to permanently stay back in Badwan and Khopri to cultivate their land and be agriculturalists. These peasants are now, however, at the verge of being dispossessed and displaced from their land and houses due to KHEP construction.

Arrival of the Capital and the Process of Land-Grabbing

The KHEP, currently under construction, on Kishanganga river (also known as Neelum river in Pakistan), was envisaged by the Indian government two decades ago. Figure 4.6 presents a view of the dam construction site. It was in June 1994 when the Indian government, under the obligation of IWT, informed Pakistan that they intended to construct the dam for HEP. By constructing a 22 kilometre tunnel, which cuts across the mighty mountains of Gurez, the water of Kishanganga river would be diverted through the tunnel to Bunkote in Bandipora district, where the power station is being built to generate electricity, before the water would be released to Wular Lake, which was once considered to be Asia's largest fresh water lake (NHPC website).[9] Figure 4.7 presents a glimpse of the water diversion tunnel.

Given its location and glacier-fed water reserves in the form of Kishanganga river, which are apt for hydroelectricity generation, the Government of India through NHPC decided to develop the 330 MW

---

[9] NHPC website gives layout plan of the project. Interview with the project head of Hindustan Construction Company (HCC), which executes the project on behalf of NHPC. http://www.nhpcindia.com/.

Figure 4.6 A View of the Construction Work on Dam for HEP in Badwan
Source: Field research picture by the author.

Figure 4.7 Tunnel for Diversion of Waters from Kishanganga to Wular Lake
Source: Field research picture by the author.

HEP here, under the name of Kishanganga HEP in 1994. The actual survey for the project was done in 1997, when a team of 12 surveyors from India led by Swedish engineer Allan Svensson surveyed the area for project construction (see Figure 4.8).[10]

Three years after the survey was done, an MoU was signed between the then Chief Minister of Kashmir and the Power Minister of India on 20 July 2000, for the execution of seven power projects in Kashmir by NHPC, including Kishanganga HEP (CSC 2011). However, those who were to be affected due to these projects were not even informed or consulted before this decision was taken. People came to know about it only in the year 2002 when the then Chief Minister visited the area and had a meeting with the local people about the project. People in one voice informed the Chief Minister that they did not want to be relocated or dispossessed of their lands, therefore HEP should not be constructed there. Even though the Chief Minister insisted that they would take the land, as it is required for 'public purpose' (the most misused term, which

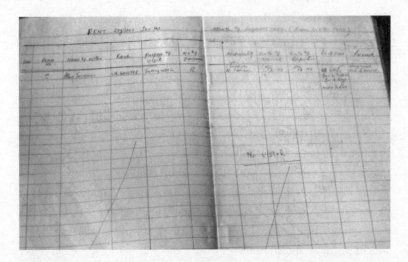

Figure 4.8 Guest Entry Registration Copy at Gurez Guest House
Mr Alisen and His 12-Member Team Had Stayed Here during the Survey
Source: Author.

---

[10] Interview with the villagers and diary report.

allows rampant and forceful land transaction in the name of 'public good'), however, after he left no progress was made in the land acquisition process or on dam construction. As the years passed, people assumed that the Government of India might have shelved the dam construction program. However, in 2009 the villagers in Badwan noticed that a massive construction work was taking place in Badwan. After inquiring about this sudden and huge scale of construction, they were told that the work on dam construction had begun and their lands have been acquired. Thus marked the intervention of capitalism and industrialization in a landlocked mountainous valley on the one hand, and worries about dislocation, dispossession, and fear of losing traditional relations, customs, and livelihoods on the other. A peasant narrated:

> Nobody asked us whether we are willing to give our land to NHPC or not. One day Additional District Commissioner came here, he just spent a few minutes here, conveyed that your land has been taken, and left. (Author interview with a peasant and village leader, June 2012)

Arbitrary control of land for 'public purpose' without prior information to the actual owners of land and property even violates the basic principles of Jammu and Kashmir Land Acquisition Act 1990. According to part II of the Act, that (a) the government needs to inform the landowners through public notices fixed at convenient places, (b) inform them through their local leaders, and (c) a notice should be published in two largest-circulation local daily newspapers. However, in this case no such procedure had been followed. Rather, the land was taken arbitrarily through extra judicial and extra economic coercion by the local administration. While NHPC claimed that it, along with the local administration, held public meetings with the peasants and took their consent before the land acquisition,[11] peasants said that neither they gave any consent nor was it sought by the administration.

[11] NHPC was questioned on 4 April 2013, through Right to Information (RTI) Act 2009, whether they have consulted the affected peasants during the land acquisition process or not.

Within this realm, the people of Badwan and Khopri did not only lose their private lands but also their customary lands, forestlands, and other 'non-private lands', which have become major targets of contemporary land-grabs. Thus what comes out of the land rights attained through conventional land reforms are not sufficient for preventing land-grabs, because land-grabbing takes place even in countries where drastic land reforms were executed, for example India, Brazil, and China (Borras and Franco 2012). Moreover, conventional land reforms meant the 'redistribution of landownership from large private landowners to small peasants farmers and landless agricultural workers, whereby emphasis is given on the redistribution of wealth' (Griffin et al. 2002: 279–90). This redistribution gives land to the landless, but most of the land in the world is: state, public, forestry, grazing, and so on. These community, forestry, state, and other non-private lands are now targets of the land-grabbers (Borras and Franco 2012). Land-grabs in Gurez reflect this phenomenon (we shall discuss about that in the next chapter).

***

Right from the fifth century AD, Kashmiri peasantry was engaged in subsistent agriculture like their counterparts in the other parts of the world. The peasantry, even though exploited by the State by imposition of taxes, which varied from regime to regime, however, had an ownership of land (excluding in the period of Dogra regime); which they could sell, lease out, gift, inherit, or transfer to any person based on their choice. However, the peasantry lost the ownership rights when the Dogras bought the state, including its dependencies from the British in 1846 under the Treaty of Amritsar. Dogras declared all the private property rights as null and void, and controlled their ownership on everything, thus turning the land owning class into serfs. This class was highly exploited by leaving just a meagre amount of food for their survival; rest of the produce was taken away by the Dogra regime, through landlords and intermediaries. As the exploitation crossed its limits, it created political awakening among the people, and led to the formation of the political party, Muslim Conference, later known as the National Conference, which after coming to power in

1948, led the most sweeping land reforms in the region. Not only were land reforms done in a smooth manner, they also paved the way for future mutual peaceful coexistence of former landlord and tenants, as these land reforms provided land to the landless, besides tenants. However, these land reforms did not prove to be of much help to the Shia sect of Muslims who were discouraged by their Aghas (religious clerics) from taking the land. Nevertheless, as peasants got the land, they started taking part in multiple livelihoods, which increased not only their income but also created mobility of people. This resulted in many people of the Gurez region opting for modern education in Srinagar city, which guaranteed them jobs in the government sector. Over the years many people from Badwan and Khopri villages settled in Srinagar or Bandipora, and thus created an absentee landlord class. This absentee landlord class, because of their access to the corridors of power, takes decisions on behalf of the poor in the villages.

Nevertheless, people were still living in peaceful coexistence which changed when the arrival of capital led to the dispossession and displacement of the Badwan and Khopri peasants. These displacements and dispossessions not only alienated people from their land, but also created further extra–community divisions among them. Grabbing and control of private property lands in Gurez by the capital, deconstructs the global notion that it is due to the absence of property rights of people over their land that the governments/corporations are able to control land. Governments 'acquires and controls' the land for the 'public purpose' despite people having ownership rights over their land. Yet, land tenure rights in Badwan and Khopri do not show that merely having rights will put an end to land-grabs, as the government would still take land for 'public purpose', despite people having ownership rights over their land.

5   Development-Induced Dispossession, Displacement, and Embedded Power Relations

After discussing the foundations of the process of land-grabbing in Badwan and Khopri in the last chapter, the class dynamics of land control, the role of elites, processes of land-grabbing and its fallouts on the people and local ecology will be examined in this chapter. There is a huge body of literature on development-induced displacement (see for example, Cernea 2007, 1997, 1990; Das 1996; Dwivedi 1997; Levien 2013; Scudder 1991; Terminski 2013). This literature categorizes the phenomena as a necessary evil or inevitable outcome of development, and thus argues to minimize the adverse impact of these projects on people. At the same time, critical Development Studies scholars see displacement as a manifestation of crisis in development. These scholars question the very basic idea of development and argue that 'extractivism' and development-induced displacement has always helped a powerful minority and neglected the interests of majority. Within this body of literature, one of the main approaches of understanding the problems arising due to displacement is the 'risk-model' promulgated by Michael Cernea (1990). This model points out that, in the absence of a prognosis or poorly managed rehabilitation plan, the displaced are facing eight risks: landlessness, joblessness, homelessness, marginalization, food insecurity, increased morbidity, loss of access to common property resources, community disarticulation. While 'risk-model' becomes a very important starting point for understanding the major impacts caused by displacements, however, as is shown in this chapter, for understanding the development-induced displacement and dispossessions and their impacts on the socio-economic and cultural fabric of society it is crucial to understand the power dynamics, and the process through which these displacements and dispossessions occur, who gets to decide/define what is 'risk' and what is 'safe' or 'certain'. Furthermore, an attempt is made to go beyond Cernea's 'risk-model', as the model itself is not (a) exhaustive enough to explain the process of contemporary land-grabbing, and (b) due to Cernea's 'reformist-managerial' ideological standpoint, which sees displacement as inevitable for economic development, and focuses on how to minimize the problems arising during resettlement process (Terminski 2013), and ignores the indigenous peoples right to land and right to move.

Within this background, the chapter begins with introducing the agrarian class structure of the battlefield—Badwan and Khopri. It goes on to explain the elite influence—who gets to decide and how? How absentee landlords take decisions on behalf of the subsistent peasantry and on yet another layer, it explains the inter-dependence of the poor with the elites and vice-versa. At the same time it also discusses peasant narratives about subordination, subalternity, and powerlessness, and at the end, control on lands. The next section of the chapter explains the process of having and losing. It mainly explains the peasants' interpretations of losses caused by dispossession and displacements. It also brings together, the viewpoints of the state, corporate, and the political parties on the micro picture of who gets what and how.

The chapter then goes on to explain how HEP's construction caused the destruction of ecology and how peasants lost the rights on common property resources. It further explains how the HEP construction affects water bodies, forests, and pasture areas, which are home to many species of birds, fisheries, animals, and the people who have dependence on these community property resources. Further, the chapter explains the concept of how land-grabbing leads to the phenomenon where land is needed but labour is not. It stresses on how peasants are exploited in the name of employment, by politicians and the corporation. The chapter ends with customary concluding remarks regarding the topics discussed.

Class Dynamics, Elite Influence, and Land Control

In Badwan, the land where the first truckloads of material for the construction of dam was unloaded, and trucks were parked, belonged to two big clans of the village—Samoons and Lones—most of them absentee landlords. An interesting question to ask would be—why the corporation took land from village elites first and why did the latter (absentee landlords) not resist and use their power to halt the land acquisition process? Some people in Badwan believe that the corporation purposely took the land of elites first, so that it becomes easy for them to take the land of less influential people later. Others believe that it is the village elites and absentee landlords who willingly gave their land first, as they were not cultivating it. However, what comes out is, that the land of the absentee landlords, which the corporation initially took to establish its base, was taken on rent until the land acquisition process was complete, and this land is still paid a rent of 9,000 rupees (around USD 150) per kanal per month. While those who gave their lands on rent argue, that they just gave their land on rent on a monthly basis and did not negotiate, felicitate, or pave the way for land acquisition process, economically marginalized people like Ganais feel that it was tacit support, approval, and felicitation of land-grabs by the village elites and absentee landlords, that made the completion of the process easier.

Absentee landlords in Badwan either give their land to the peasants for cultivation or keep it uncultivated; therefore renting out land to NHPC was more profitable than lending it to a peasant for potato or pulse cultivation. However, as the corporation got control of land of elites and absentee landlords, rest of the village became helpless. For them the only influential people they knew, and could have been approached to resist the land acquisition process, were the ones who supported and facilitated the land-grabs. Ahsan Mir, father of four, who owns 10 kanals of land responded to the question, 'Why did they not resist land-grabs, if they were not happy', with anger, and said, 'We had only access to our elites and absentee landlords, who are not only landowners here but are holding big government positions as well. When they gave the land first, we had no other option except to give up our lands'.

Within this background, an analysis of land-grabbing in Badwan and Khopri has to consider the class dynamics of these villages. In general, the villages of Badwan and Khopri represent a class of subsistence-oriented peasant family system. Every family owns a portion of land and cattle—sheep, cows, horses, and donkeys. Women work in the field, and men, apart from cultivating their own land, work with the army as porters, and with the Hindustan Construction Company (HCC) as helpers. Some of them are also employed in government jobs while the rest of them are daily wage labourers. Every family member works in the family farm, baring children who provide a helping hand to their parents at the time of harvesting. After securing enough food to meet their needs for a year, peasants in Badwan and Khopri sell parts of their produce to buy clothing, medicine, and other necessities of life, including books and payment of education fee for their children. In this scheme, the family in these villages is, as Scott (1976) describes, 'a unit of consumption and a unit of production'. However, like other hill people with small arable landholdings, people in Badwan and Khopri engage in multiple livelihoods for survival, thus the peasant society no longer remains monolithic.

For example, Zona Baigum, 70, has five kids. Three of them are employed in the local government and two are students in a local school. She owns 50 Kanals (2.5 hectares) of land—a landlord in Kashmiri context. On the other hand, Zouja Baigum 65, years old, has only one Child who works in the police department. Zouja owns only 10 Kanals of land. Similarly, Satar Ganai, 70 years old, father of two daughters, owns five Kanals of land. Village Sarpanch, Samad lone, father of 12 kids, owns 45 Kanals of land. Similar is the situation with other people. Overall every family in the village has *milkiyati* (private ancestral) land, a *rakh* (customary land for grazing). Besides they raise horses, cows, and sheep and have a modest house to live in. (Group interview, Badwan dam site, June 2012)

Landownership in Badwan and Khopri is highly skewed. People, like the Samoons, own more land than other castes, such as Ganais. Landownership coupled with livelihood occupation determines the socio-economic status of a person, which is a crucial factor in the decision-making process (Figure 5.1). Samoons, Lones, and Mirs are among the well-to-do clans. Ganais are on the lowest ladder of economic status. Since the Ganais' socio-economic status as compared to others is relatively low, the benefits they yield from the government or other agencies are also lower than other castes, primarily because they do not have power and means to negotiate. As observed by Long (2004), power here does not have to be looked at through hegemonic control, hierarchy, the capacity

Figure 5.1   Interview with a 'Marginalized' Peasant Family
Source: Aijaz Mir.

to act, and the position one holds in government or elsewhere; rather, it has to be seen through the social status, reputation, educational level, and the capacity to resist and negotiate. Unequal power relations are the outcome of unequal household income in these areas. Ganais do not have the position, capacity, educational level, and socio-economic status to sit across the table to negotiate the terms of their land deal. Rather, it is the Samoons, and a few among the Lones and Mirs who decide on their behalf and on behalf of other socio-economically disadvantaged people. They cannot oppose the decision either; as they are what they call themselves 'chote log' (under-privileged people) or the subaltern class; as they have to maintain a social cohesion and be obedient to enjoy the share of government welfare schemes, which comes through elites. What comes out, is that, their inaction is an intervention that reinforces the status quo.

Here again, when it is a question of enjoying benefits from government schemes, such as reservation in government jobs, educational institutions, out of turn promotions in government services, funds for development, and scholarships which are meant for people living in far-flung areas, it is the absentee landlords who are the first beneficiaries.

Quite akin to what Scott (1985) observes, elites in peasant societies do exploit and undermine the very being of people from the lower strata, yet they have to use their services in farming and during festivals. Although exploitative, here the upper class and the lower strata enjoy a relationship of interdependence.

To survive and provide proper food, shelter, health care, and education to their kids, people opt for different livelihoods. It is their skills, educational qualification, the property they own, and the position they hold in the State administration, which determine and define their power and influence in the decision-making process. Thus village elites and affluent people—mostly absentee landlords—who have partially-migrated to Srinagar or Bandipora, but have houses in Badwan and Khopri, occupy high government positions.

It is within this background that when the state decided to take land for the Kishanganga HEP, absentee landlords and village elites secured their interests first and then covertly supported the land-grabbing process.

Nevertheless, people started demanding from the corporation and from local government officials as to why they were not consulted at the time of the land acquisition process. Villagers were told that the decision about land acquisition was done with the consent of village leaders. Upon inquiring about who was taken in confidence when the land acquisition process was taking place, people came to know it was only a few people, including the then Divisional Commissioner (regional administrative head of the government) who also hails from Badwan, along with two Lone families and one leader from the National Conference, who took the decision of giving the land to NHPC. The following three statements of peasants make official apathy, elite influence, and peasant oppression in land acquisition process clearer:

> Nobody asked us whether we are willing to give our land to NHPC or not. One day Additional District Commissioner came here, he just spent a few minutes here, conveyed that your land has been taken, and left. (Author interview with Majnoon Mir, a village leader, May 2012)

> There are those elite people, government officers, who live in Srinagar, they decided about the land. What could we do? We said, we will not give the land but they said, we have order from above [Higher Authorities] … so we will take the land. (Author interview with a 70-year-old peasant, Hassan Ganai, June 2012)

> The agreement was decided with elites not with us. They signed the agreement in Srinagar not here in Badwan. Those elites already live in Bandipora or Srinagar, but they also have houses registered here … they have land here too. If they get compensation they will put this money in bank. Unlike us, they do not need to build a new house. If the government builds a house for them, they will get another house. For them it is a great deal. They are happy with the project but we are not. (Author interview with the village sarpanch [leader] of Badwan, June 2011)

Peasants in Gurez often do not have access or the means to visit district headquarters in Bandipora, or the state summer capital Srinagar, to fight against problems related to governance and other issues that are to be addressed by the state. It is their helplessness that they have to depend on the village elites or absentee landlords without whom they will not get benefit of government schemes. It is thus their influence on people and their covert or overt support to the corporation that made land acquisition process very smooth for the government. However, they often make visits to sub-district magistrate's HCC offices in Daver to demand compensation. But these visits often turn out to be a futile exercise, as they have to wait for hours, sometimes for days, to meet the concerned officials, who either do not come to office frequently or refuse to meet them.

With state, corporation, and absentee landlords joining hands to control land, peasants in Badwan and Khopri were pressurized to accept land acquisition deals. They were given motivations through promises of adequate compensation, development, employment, better housing, and education for their children. When the corporation started construction, the peasants, despite assurances of compensation and benefits, started protesting against the corporation. The company increased compensations—along the lines of recent tactics of corporations to lure people with more compensation, which includes fulltime employment to one member of the dispossessed and displaced family, scholarships to school-going children, and construction of five-bedroom houses in Srinagar or Bandipora. Local HCC officials, such as engineer Chuhan, who I had met for the first time in the year 2002 at KHEP dam site, said that the peasants want to exploit the corporation. 'This land was worth nothing, we are giving them Rs 6 lakhs per kanal. Isn't that too much for this land?' Without waiting for my response, he continued saying, 'people here just want easy money'. Chuhan was echoing the line that many Indians hold about Kashmir and Kashmiris; that they are lazy and survive on Indian money, without contributing much to the 'national income'.

Nevertheless, not assuaged by verbal assurances by the corporation, in November 2011 'peasant representatives' (village elites) held a meeting with the District Commissioner (DC) of Bandipora and regional head of NHPC, where NHPC reiterated that they are committed to provide monitory compensation, jobs, and housing to the effected people. Village 'representatives' went back to Gurez and informed the people about the meeting and the promises NHPC has made with them. People patiently waited for the corporation to fulfil its promises to them, however, when they did not receive any communication from the corporation for over a month they went to meet the corporation representatives stationed in Gurez. People had gone with a hope to get a final word from the corporation about the compensation, however what they heard was shocking to them. They found the HCC officials there, who informed them that NHPC has outsourced the construction work of the dam to HCC. This was a tactical move of the corporation, thereby relieving itself from the responsibility of facing peasants who were fighting for justice. For HCC it was just another contract to build infrastructure for the energy security of the country. They were not against providing 'employment', albeit temporary, to the effected people. Since HCC contract finishes with the completion of the dam and power project construction, they will be answerable to none after the HEP becomes functional. For NHPC, dealing with aggrieved peasants would not be a problem, as they would blame HCC for violating commitment with the peasants. It is a win-win situation for both the companies. While HCC officials in Gurez and Badwan are the face of dam construction, NHPC on the other hand, has negligible presence. Therefore, people often go to HCC office to press for the demands.

While the promises of compensations are yet to be met, it is the cost and benefits of this project, which have become a major debate.

Dynamics of Dispossession and Gain

Peasants in Badwan and Khopri own and are dependent on common property resources and personal property resources. As stated above, almost everyone in Badwan and Khopri owns a portion of land on which they grow maize, wheat, potato, pulses, garlic, and condiments, besides raising sheep, horses, chicken, and cows. For those who do not have any other source of income except farming, they sell agricultural produce outside Gurez and in turn buy rice, the staple food, and some spices from the market. The produce is sold outside only after evaluating the 'safety-first' mechanism (Scott 1976).

However, as the construction of the dam and HEP has commenced, so has the peasants' worries about displacement, dispossession, losing the self-sufficiency of food, and the period of uncertainty begun. In Figure 5.2 a peasant of Badwan explains to the author about his fears and fallouts of HEP on Gurez and Gurezees. The impacts of the HEP construction on the economic, social, cultural, and traditional ethos are the major concerns shared by the peasants. While the corporation and the government see the impacts of the land-grabbing through compensation lens, whereby the land deals are seen as necessary for the 'development' and 'resettlement' in terms of jobs and housing, provided to the affected. However, the question of 'whose' development, and the whole argument of adequate compensation just by looking at the market value of land is problematic. Numerous studies (for example, Borras and Franco 2012; Polanyi 1944; Scott 1998; Sérgio and Sergio 2011) have questioned this framing of quantifying the value of land in terms of its productivity and ignoring the social functions and social relations of the land. Majority of peasants in Badwan and Khopri coincide in saying that the HEP construction is

Figure 5.2   Interaction with a Peasant in Badwan
Source: Athar Parvez.

a move that uproots them and has turned them from self-sufficient, self-reliant households to being dependents on market forces.

Mohammad Siraj, a village elite in Badwan, explains the importance of land, and the fear of losing the homeland:

> Zamindar [farmer/peasant] is like a king. I have everything in my house— sheep, chicken, vegetables, rice, wheat, almost everything. We do not want to leave from here. We want to stay here. We do not want money or anything. We are self-sufficient. We want to live like this. They [corporation] say, they will give us enough compensation for our land and houses. What will we do to this money, which they give us as compensation? Even if they give us huge money, but can money compensate the loss of losing my childhood memories, which I have with my home? Can money buy me this fresh air there in the city? Can money last forever? More importantly, everyone here would be moved to the outskirts of Srinagar city, where everything is many times more expensive than here. The money they give us as compensation, it will not last even for a year. (Author interview with Yousuf, a peasant from Khopri village, May 2012)

In the absence of 'state welfare' system in Kashmir it is the communitarian social capital in hilly areas—as a part of reciprocal system, that works in times of need. However, as displacement would take place, people fear losing ties with other people as well as the culture of reciprocity. The closely bonded culture of sharing grief and happiness not only with their neighbours inside a village, but also with their acquaintances in adjacent villages is what they fear of losing after their displacement. This is what I observed during one of my visits to Khopri. Upon arriving in the village, I could hardly find anyone inside the village. After inquiring from a young boy about the absence of people in the village, I was told that a young boy from an adjacent village in Wanpora—a village two kilometres away from Badwan and five kilometres away from Khopri—had died in the morning, so everybody—men and women—have gone there to offer condolences. After spending few hours in the village, I decided to move back to Daver in the afternoon. On my way back I met many people from Khopri who were returning from the deceased's home. All of them were in grief.

Sadness was visible on their faces. It looked like they had lost someone of their own. While crossing the footbridge that connects Khopri with Daver I met Haji Sahab and few other people from Khopri. Before I could ask him whether they were also returning from the funeral, Haji Sahab looked at me and said, 'come, let's go back and have tea at my home. We are just returning from funeral of a boy who died in a road accident. We all were there'. Upon asking if they knew the deceased and his family, Haji replied, 'it does not matter, we all are one family and one clan here'. Imran, a young man who was accompanying Haji interjected and said:

> Today you cannot find people here in this village. Majority of us had gone to Wanpora to the house of Hassan Mir, whose son died in a car accident yesterday. Here it is our culture to share happiness and grief with the people of the village, as well as whole area. Nobody goes to work today, the streets are empty, the houses are empty, and do you know why?

I replied by saying, 'No, I don't know'. He answered, 'Because people feel that they have lost someone from their own family. Even though most of us did not know the deceased, but it is the community culture which keeps us intact'. Hashim, another youth interrupted, 'Look, It is not city culture, where people live separately, they do not know their neighbour ... here we live with mutual peaceful coexistence. This is what we are going to lose once we will be evicted from our homeland' (Group interaction, Khopri, June 2012).

Peasants in Badwan and Khopri are living in a constant fear of losing their land and houses, culture, tradition and brotherhood. However, for the absentee landlords, acquisition of the land at such a price is a fortune. They give their agricultural land for cultivation to Ganais and other relatively poorer families, and in return get a 50 per cent share of the produce. They have also lost cultural bonding with the place. They are the ones who own most of the land and therefore get more compensation. For them it is the material value of the land that matters, not its social importance.

Likewise, Badwan and Khopri's younger generation, that resides or studies in Srinagar city, seem to be fed-up with road blockages of six months and seem to be tempted by city life and modern job market.

For them, dispossession from their land and displacement from their homes is in a way a blessing in disguise to leave the village for good and settle in the city. This generation of people, on the one hand, do not feel tempted to do farming, as it would not give them what they call 'good social status', on the other hand, the small land holding also forces them to opt for multiple livelihoods as they cannot sustain with what they produce on the field. This is quite akin to what Scott (1976) observed, 'peasants with smaller land holding would opt for alternative livelihoods for their survival'. Here the peasants with smaller land holding with meagre amount of arable land, have been found opting for multiple 'non-farm' livelihoods, which is also quite a reflection of people living in mountainous areas (Jean-Yves et al. 2012). Keeping the challenges in mind, most of the youth of Badwan and Khopri wants to opt for government jobs in the city.

During the research process, I delivered a couple of lectures in a local higher secondary school. In one of my lectures in Gurez, I asked students of the girls' higher secondary school, and the students of the degree college, to write down future plans of their lives, and what do they want to do after they complete their education. Surprisingly, 95 per cent of the students wrote that they wanted to pursue government jobs in the city. Taking up a government job in the city would entail leaving behind rural and peasant life. This is quite a reflection of why a peasant's children do not want to be peasants. This phenomenon of aspiration for government and 'non-farm' city jobs causes, initially, migration for education, which later turns into labour migration.

Contrary to the young generation, Badwan and Khopri's older generation, including women, is most averse to the forcible migration and dispossession from their land and houses. They see this as a move to uproot them from where they have lived for decades and therefore, find themselves incompatible with city life. Quite akin to what Cernea (2007) describes, development-induced displacement leads to marginalization and loss of existing acquired skills. The women of Badwan and Khopri, majority of whom are illiterate, also see themselves as being thrown out of their homes and deprived of their only livelihood; farming. Since majority of women here have not got any formal education, therefore they are not acclimatized with any other language except Sheena—their native language. Some of them, like Zona, mother of four, has not even been to Srinagar. Others have made occasional visits—one or two times—a year for health checkups. Despite spending almost 98 per cent of their time to take care of home, cultivating food in the field, grazing cattle, bringing fire wood from forests, they say, they are in absolute love with everything in Gurez. They can't find such pure *aab we hawa*, literally meaning air, water, and climate, but figuratively includes the whole environment, surrounding, brotherhood, and society. Ironically, they were never consulted—neither by the authorities nor by the male heads of the family—when the decisions about the land deals were made. Fehti, a 75-year-old woman, who has spent her entire life in Badwan explains the meaning of loss: 'I do not know where we will live. We were told we have to leave from here. But nobody asked us [women]. How can I live in a place where I do not have my own culture, language', she sobbed. 'I have never been to Srinagar or Bandipora', she emphasized. Thus land-grabs here do not only undermine the economic and social function of land but also the 'cultural significance' of it (De Schutter 2011).

Amidst this uncertainty about where to live, where to work, how to cope with the new life/culture, jobs, and so on, shared by women, men, and elderly; some village elites in Badwan and Khopri, who otherwise are indifferent to the problems faced by the lower class and often collide with the state to covertly suppress the voices of lower class, also fear losing their respect, identity, and possibly being identified as 'strangers' or 'refugees' and psychologically marginalized in the city—the place where they would be 'resettled'. A village elite put it this way:

> I am a Jagirdar's [landlord's] son. Today I can call or even *yell* at anyone here in my village. But now I am forced to leave, I will lose all my identity, power, and respect. There are two refugee families from Pakistan in this village. I tell you honestly, we do not talk to them properly. We treat them as outsiders. Two days ago I was talking with few friends in the village and all of us started ridiculing ourselves for treating the two families whose ancestors have migrated from Pakistan as *other*. We never realized, what it means to leave your homeland and live in a different locality. While those two families had come here by choice, yet they are facing difficulties.

In our case it is worst as we are being forcibly displaced. We all will be refugees soon. (Author interview with Yosuf, a local political leader and village elite, July 2011. Emphasis in original conversation)

Within this realm of uncertainty about fear of losing culture, honour, and rights on their resources, village elites as a part of 'communitarian approach', fight for the community interest (Scott 1976). One thing which the village elites and lower classes share is the adverse impact the project have had on people, how it affected existing livelihoods and how in return they are getting inadequate compensation, and not even electricity.

The area, which is to produce 330 MW electricity, depends, ironically, on the electricity generated by kerosene generator provided and controlled by the Indian Army. The generator is turned on for two hours in the evening and one hour in the morning daily. Thus, out of 24 hours, Gurez gets electricity for only three hours. Khalil Lone, from Khopri, says that the benefits of these projects will be reaped by people outside Kashmir.

NHPC wants to illuminate Hindustan [India]. Neither Gurez or Bandipora nor Kashmir gets benefit of it. We are helpless; we cannot do anything against NHPC or Indian state. Just we have to accept the fact that we have to leave from here. (Author interview with a peasant, Khalil Lone, April 2011)

For Khalil Lone, there are other concerns too; such as hike in land prices near the dam site. This is quite akin to what Sérgio Sauer and Sergio Pereira Leite (2011) have observed in Brazil where that land prices shoot up due to land-grabs. Land-grabs for hydropower projects built in hilly and mountainous areas, such as in Gurez, where the arable land is scarce, lead to hike in land prices in adjacent areas, thereby making it unaffordable for people to purchase land even for house construction.

At the same time, the construction of 'temporary' huts for HCC workers, has changed the landscape of the area. People are no longer able to identify their lands amidst this arbitrary control on private spaces, and its fallouts on the peasantry. It is important to note here that the peasantry in mountainous areas is much dependent on the community property resources and customary resources for their subsistence, which shall become part of our discussion in the next section.

Paradise Turns Hell: Control on Common Property Resources

'An Posh Tele Yale Wane Posh' (food will last, as long as forest lasts), reciting the widely used saying of a thirteenth century Kashmiri saint, Sheik Noor-u-din Wali, sitting on veranda of his house, Khalil Lone, 79, of Badwan goes nostalgic, explaining in his quavering voice the beautiful and memorable times he has spent in his village. He takes pride in mentioning that many foreign and Indian tourists including India's first Prime Minister Jawaharlal Nehru with his daughter Indira Gandhi, who later become the Prime Minister of India, had visited this small beautiful valley. 'The Mughal emperor said, Kashmir is a paradise on earth, I would say, Gurez is the heart of that paradise, in terms of its natural beauty and habitat ... but now NHPC is turning paradise into hell', he says to me.[1]

The ongoing construction of a dam and 24-kilometre long tunnel from Badwan, Gurez to Kralpora, Bandipora, which pierces through the lush green Gurez Mountains, has caused the destruction of ecology. According to Mr Chuhan, the company had to cut hundreds of trees for this major project of 'national importance'. Chuhan brags about the machinery the company has used to construct this tunnel. Upon asking whether cutting down the trees is bad for the environment, he calls it a 'price worth to be paid' for the projects that will provide electricity to the thousands of households, factories, and companies outside in India. Peasants, on the other hand, see cutting down of thousands of lush green Deodar trees as *looth* (plunder) by the company. The forest area now wears a deserted look. Imran Ahmad, a college student, explains the adverse impacts of the HEP:

> Our land has been ruined because of this project. Our forests have been destructed. We do not have a place to graze cattle; the pathways are

---

[1] Author interview with Khalil lone of Badwan, August 2012.

destroyed. We do not have clean drinking water and pure water for irrigation anymore. (Author interview with Imran Ahmad, Badwan, August 2012)

As the dam construction has started, it has not only affected those people whose land and houses will get submerged, but has also majorly affected common property resources on which people living in nearby villages are dependent. For example, to divert the waters, HCC created tunnels with the use of chemicals. As a result Kishanganga waters not only got polluted, but also became contaminated and haramful for human consumption and irrigation of agricultural fields. The otherwise most clean and purified water for human consumption has turned so harmful that thousands of trout fish died in Madhumati Stream, in which, the water of Kishanganga is released (Ajmal 2012b; Saleem 2012). Similarly Badwan's Throutkole (trout stream), home of trout fish, does not have trout anymore. As the water got polluted, trout fish started disappearing. People started sharing concerns about the impact of HEP construction on water. There were protests against the ecological destruction followed by extensive media reports. Alarmed by rising public opposition about the environmental impacts of the project, the Jammu and Kashmir assembly constituted a three-member legislative committee of lawmakers, headed by M.Y. Tarigami, to access the impacts of HEP on environment. The committee found that the project has adversely affected the environment. As the committee report grabbed headlines, with Kashmir's leading daily, *Greater Kashmir*, publishing a story on this report on 12 August 2012 titled, 'Environment Ignored in Kishanganga Execution', it was already a public debate. The committee report gave handle to civil society actors in Kashmir to corner NHPC for violating norms. I interviewed Tarigami at his Gupkar residence in Srinagar, soon after he returned back from Gurez. The otherwise cheerful Tarigami was visibly upset about what he described as 'destruction' that he has seen. He went on to say:

During the construction of the dam and tunnel for water diversion, huge environment loss has taken place, which is beyond compensation. The corporations need to be responsible for environment protection. This is more important here as people's livelihoods depend on these forests and other natural resources, which are being destroyed due to the HEP construction. (Author interview, August 2012)

Seeing the pollution of water, people in Bandipora, where the diverted water gets released, staged protests against the corporation in 2012. Following the reports, National Institute of Technology (NIT) Srinagar did water testing, and found that the water had been contaminated and was no longer fit for human consumption and washing (Ajmal 2012b). Similarly, another report 'An Environmental Impact Assessment (EIA)' done by Delhi University's Centre for Inter-Disciplinary Studies of Mountain and Hill Environment, argued that the dam construction in Gurez would endanger several animal species, such as the snow leopard and black bear in the area, besides affecting Himalayan plants (Parvaiz 2011).

The HEP construction is causing water contamination and deforestation, at the same time, diversion of the Kishanganga waters that are to be released to Madumathi stream and finally to Wular Lake, is believed to cause a huge problem like floods in Kashmir. The lake that has already shrunk due to encroachments by local communities in Bandipora, causing floods in the downstream areas during springtime, is expected to pose even higher threats. Since the Kishanganga waters are being diverted to the lake, it may now flood these areas in north Kashmir.

The diversion, reallocation, and control of water by the corporation for its benefits does not only make it a clear-cut water-grabbing case (Franco et al. 2013; Mehta et al. 2012), but the contamination of water through the construction of tunnel violates the human rights of the people—access to clean water and sanitation—and causes harm to many species of birds and fishes which live in the fresh waters.

The contamination of water and control on the common property resources has direct bearing on the common peasantry in Badwan and Khopri. Here what is noticed is quite akin to what Cernea (2007) observes; that the control on common property resources creates an income gap for the affected people. Peasants in Badwan and Khopri get significant share of their income by edible wild vegetables and other edible forest products, firewood, grazing cattle in the pasture areas, condiments grown in the forests, and other medicinal plants.

The corporation does not pay any compensation for the loss of access to common property resources, which are a major source of income generation for the tribal people. Control-grabbing of common property resources has direct affects on the income levels of peasants, and it leads to the loss of access to some other public services such as school (Mathur 1998). Yet, when we see the fallout of the HEP construction beyond the economic prism, and try to understand the social and cultural functions of the common/customary property resources, a peasant's statement, reproduced below, sums it up:

> God has given us land; to work on it and it would yield us fruits. In this paradise called Gurez, where the green forests, the fresh water, the clean air, and abundance of land to graze our cattle are Gods vouchsafe for us. We tried to protect, but the corporation snatched it from us. How can somebody compensate such a loss, it cannot be compensated. It can't be. (Author interview with Hilal Lone, Khopri, June 2011)

Peasants often mention their relation with land. Land, water, and air in this place are seen as God's *Ammanat* (vouchsafe) and their protection as *ibadat* (prayer). Peasants' dependence on these natural resources and protection of the same for their personal benefits might be seen as visible posturing on part of peasants to preserve the source of their income, and may not necessarily reflect their care for ecological preservation. Yet when we look at the history of ecological preservation in Kashmir in general, and Gurez in particular, people have always been concerned about the preservation of nature, which is quite a reflection of present day Gurez as well—baring the HEP construction areas. This goes against the notion which sees environment protection and preservation as prophesy of the western and rich countries. In this analysis, poorer countries are being judged as not being concerned about environment protection. An interesting account of this can derived from Luster, in the following lines:

> If you look at the countries that are interested in environmentalism, or at the individuals who support environmentalism within each country, one is

struck by the extent to which environment is an interest of the upper middle class. Poor countries and individuals simply aren't interested. (Luster
1980: 104–5)

In this scheme, poor people are thought to be more interested in
procuring food and shelter, while concerns about nature come into
consideration only when the basic needs are met (Guha 2006). Now,
if we judge the peasants of Badwan and Khopri with Luster's yard-
stick, then people should not be concerned about nature and natural
resources, given their economic conditions. They should have destroyed
ecology, water resources, pasturelands, killed birds, and wild animals,
irrespective of their dependence on them. However, here the story is
different, not only in the current context whereby the people do exploit
the natural resources for their survival, but they also preserve them. If
one tree is cut, ten more are planted, unlike capitalist industrial projects
such as HEP construction, which lead to control of common property
resources. This wave of violent appropriation of common resources by
capital for its survival, in which water, which was previously outside the
capital's orbit, has become a battlefield for a new round of accumulation
(Harvey 2003). While environmentalism in the West emerged in the
late nineteenth century, the practice and preaching of ecological preservation reflected in this widely known couplet of thirteenthth century
Kashmiri saint, Sheikh-ul-Alam, Sheik Noor-u-din's 'an posh tele yale
wen posh' (roughly translated as, food will last as long as forests last),[2]
presents a different theory of ecological preservation. Therefore, Luster,
as argued by Guha, had on the one hand failed to pay attention to the
environmental movements around the world which were quite vibrant,
and on the other hand, he had fallen in the trap of what Guha calls
'disciplinary chauvinism'—'The belief the social and cultural changes are
the simple by-product of economic changes' (2006: 2–3).

Peasants in Badwan and Khopri take pride in having preserved
their water bodies, ecology and dense forests, pasture areas and other

---

[2] *Kulyate I Sheikh Ul Alam*, translated by Abu Naeem. Published by Sheikh
Mohammad Usman and Sons, Srinagar, 2012.

common property resources. They were self-sufficient and were unaware of any climate change led water scarcity. This is quite akin to what the 2006 Human Development Report[3] claimed—'water scarcity is socially constructed and failed policies, not of environmental characteristics of different regions.' Nevertheless, with the intrusion of capital, the negotiations between NHPC and the State of Kashmir about HEP were taking place, but the issue of water usage was never discussed, nor was the issue of common property discussed. The State neither asked the corporation to pay for the water charges, nor did it assess the impact of dam and tunnel construction on ecology and common property resources of the peasantry. The economic advisor to the state government stated:

> For electricity generation you need three resources: Land, Water, and Capital. Kahsmiris are providing the NHPC land and water. Land is given just for meager amount, water is given free. Yet, what we get is just 12 percent royalty of our resources. The corporation is exploiting our natural resources and what we get in return is nothing. (Author interview with a professor of economics and advisor to the state government, August 2011)

With the arbitrary control on common property resources resulting in a direct impact on the peasantry and destruction of ecology, it is the issue of compensation, in terms of employment, invoked by the corporation, to keep the aggravated peasantry in the hope that the alternative livelihoods in terms of life long employment would serve their interests better. In the next section, we shall discuss the issue of livelihoods and how the promises about jobs have proved to be bogus.

When Land is Needed People are Not

If one has to find the most common ground/claim between the national/subnational and the multinational corporations regarding the benefits

[3] UNDP, Human Development Report 2006. For the background papers, see http://hdr.undp.org/en/reports/global/hdr2006/papers/.

they would provide to the local people in lieu of the land, one claim would always top the list—jobs. On the contrary, contemporary land deals in the world suggest that the promises of jobs are never fulfilled (Li 2011). Same is the story with Kishanganga HEP. Right from the assessment of the land for the construction of HEP, the corporation along with the state government, made a promise to the people that those who were to be affected during dispossession and displacement, one member of their family would be given fulltime employment in the corporation. Full-time employment with the corporation was projected as a lifetime opportunity for the peasants. A narrative was also built to project, that since agricultural production is not sustainable there, getting employment with the corporations is better than on-farm livelihoods. Non-local employees of the corporation would go a step further and describe jobs offered to the local people—who for them were unskilled, lazy, and uncooperative—as a favour to them by the corporation. Mr Chuhan described the role of his corporation (HCC) as that of empowering the local community. Chuhan vociferously argued that HEP construction would build work culture among the otherwise lazy people. Furthermore, the incomes generated by the people through HEP and by taking compensation of their land, will allow them to go to the city, get educated there, live and have a much better life. Thus HEP wore the 'good' corporate mask to empower Kashmir's youth and Kashmir economy through education and employment generation.

However, locals believe it is the corporation which has been exploiting them. Mohammad Subhan who has been working with HCC feels the corporation is disrespecting them and their work by saying that they are lazy. 'If we are lazy, then who is working inside the tunnels? Who is constructing this dam?' he lamented. 'One of my neighbours, a young boy, recently died in January under a snow avalanche while clearing the road. Was he lazy?' an angry Subhan asks. Zaheer, a young boy, who was working for HCC had died in a snow avalanche. He is remembered as a brave boy in the village, who was committed to his work. His family, however, feels the corporation has not even given compensation for his loss or recognized and appreciated his sacrifice for the company.

Nevertheless, Chuhan was not wrong in saying that the corporation has been providing jobs to the local people. Zaheer, Subhan, Imran, and many others who I have talked to, were working with HCC, but only as casual labourers. Since the project construction was happening in a very remote area where outside labourers would have been expensive and difficult to manage, providing employment to the locals helped the larger interest of the corporation to find cheap and productive labour. In this case providing employment to the people would also make them honest in the eyes of the people whom they had promised to provide employment. Providing jobs to the local peasants would also ensure their allegiance to the corporation and guarantee of not disrupting the construction work. But more importantly, local people knew the terrain, the geography of the area and were acclimatized with the local environment. Therefore, a sizeable number of people from the twin villages were employed as casual labourers, with few people given supervisory roles as well. However, as people handed over the papers of their land, some of them came to know that the jobs are not permanent—they were temporary and will be valid until the HEP become functional. Once they approached the corporation, the corporation and the administration asserted, that the jobs are permanent in nature. While some accepted the claim, others rejected it and argued the jobs are temporary and blamed NHPC for misleading them. Yet, there are others like Hassan Mir, from Khopri, who says that employment with the corporation cannot compensate the losses they suffered.

> I have seven sons and six daughter's, besides me and my wife. In total we are 15 people in one family. Here we would cultivate our land and live a self-sufficient life. But now, they have taken our land, and in return they promised to give us money as compensation. Moreover, they promised to provide job to one member of our family. They have also promised to give us 3-bedroom house in the outskirts of city in Srinagar. Company and government officials say we are getting enough compensation. But how can a 15-member family live in three room apartment? How can this meager amount of monthly salary (average USD 170) they offer to employees help to feed 15 member household in a city where we have to buy everything from the market—even the water. And we do not know how long that employment will last? And suppose tomorrow my son, now the only

earning hand in our family, gets married, what will happen to my other family members, in case he decides to live separately with his wife ... who will take care of me and my family? (Author interview with a peasant from Khopri, June 2011)

While the corporation's offer of providing permanent job to one member of the affected family has some takers, majority of peasants share Hassan Mir's apprehensions that a single earning hand cannot sustain a seven or eight member family—an average family size—in the city. This was also a discussion in Mushtaq's shop in Badwan. While opinions and counter opinions among the people were going on, Imran a young peasant joined the discussion and countered everyone and made them silent by saying these jobs are contractual. Imran was right, jobs provided by HCC were not permanent in nature, as the company would close its operation in Gurez after the completion of the HEP. With that, the contracts of the employees would also come to an end leading to what Tania Li (2011) calls 'dispossessed people' becoming 'surplus people' as the outcome of these land deals.

Promises of permanent jobs were not only made to the people of Badwan and Khopri, NHPC has in the past promised permanent jobs to the peasants of other areas where they have built similar power projects. For example, Uri I HEP was completed in 1997 and has been operational since then. NHPC promised the locals, that one member of the family, whose land has been acquired for the projects, will be provided a job. However, that promise was never kept.[4] Moreover, the corporation in its agreement with the government also agreed to reserve 50 per cent of all categories of staff on the project from the state of Jammu and Kashmir. However, that promise was never met either (CSC 2011). Interestingly, NHPC earns 50 per cent of its profits from the HEP projects in Kashmir but employs only a few people in its executive class. Out of 207 executive positions in Uri I, Uri II, and Kishanganga only 25 of its employees are from Kashmir. Similar is the tale of supervisory jobs, where locals are at the marginal level. For the third and fourth class positions, locals have been employed but here too they are being outnumbered by outsiders (Maqbool 2012).

---

[4] Interview with the dispossessed peasants of Boniyar Uri.

As Kashmir has the highest unemployment rate among the northern Indian states of Punjab, Haryana, Himachal Pradesh, and Delhi (*Greater Kashmir* 2013), getting employment in the region is seen as a big blessing. NHPC, with the support of local politicians, convinced people to give up their land against the monetary compensations and jobs. However, they are aware about the fact that operating a hydroelectricity projects does not require huge manpower. Iftikhar Drabu, hydroelectric engineer by profession, who has previously worked as a consultant with NHPC notes that not more than six to eight people are required for the daily operations of a HEP:

> Politicians and the corporation are making false claims of job creation. What kind of jobs will local people do in the technical project? All these claims are just to lure people to give up their land. Once they agree to give land, promises of jobs will also fade away. (Author interview, July 2012)

Exploiting peasants in the name of 'permanent/sustainable employment' is, on the one hand, a move towards linking people with the organizations and turning them, in Marx's terms, from 'owners' into 'workers'; and, on the other hand, relieving them from these jobs after the completion of the project construction. This in turn is leading to the phenomenon, where their land is needed but labour is not (Li 2011). Furthermore, the nexus between the corporation and the politicians becomes more obvious as politicians and state ministers often speak against the corporation for exploiting the resources, yet, it is the State ministers and politicians who have the authority to give or take back any project from the corporation. However, they have never taken any project back from them; instead they have given sanctions to construct more HEPs from time to time. Moreover, the bogus job creation serves the politicians in two ways: if the corporation provides some jobs, even if temporary, the local politicians use them as their successes to appease their voting constituency. However, if the corporation fails to provide such jobs they blame it publically to appease their constituencies yet again. While the promises of job creation by corporations in the contemporary land deals have been observed as misleading (Li 2011; Mishra 2011), they are more deceptive in the context of HEPs where the demand of labour is very low and non-technical labour is not needed much. In the absence of sustainability of long-term jobs in such projects, self-sufficient peasants are left jobless. With the peasant's first losing land, then jobs, it turns out to be a phenomenon where land is needed but labour is not. Yet the third dimension of it is, that while major portions of the peasants' land is taken, some patches are left, therefore it creates further problems for the peasants, where neither land is needed nor the people.

***

Development-induced displacement and dispossession in Badwan and Khopri does not only go beyond the 'routinely' impact analysis fashion, and present the class dynamics of the land-grabs of the twin villages. In the two villages, what is observed is that the elites are ruling the roost, while peasants live the life of subalternity—not just in terms of life standards, rather decision making powers, whereby the peasant's right to choose, decide, and not decide rests with the absentee landlords. This was reflected when the local administration and the corporation signed the agreement about the HEP construction. Those who were to be affected due to land, house, and water-grabbing were not even consulted. Rather, the elites (absentee landlords) decided on their behalf. Absentee landlords not only hold big government positions, but also own major portion of land. For them losing the land is not a matter, as they have already left the village. It is poor peasants who face the brunt of dispossession and expulsion. The hardships caused by land-grabs include impacts on economic resources, culture, tradition, livelihoods, common property resources, and ecology, and snatching of social ties. While initially the jobs are provided by the corporation, however, it has been observed that as the corporation completes the construction work, these workers are laid-off employees, thus creating a phenomenon where land is needed, labour is not (Li 2011). On the other hand, while peasants are displaced to hundreds of kilometres away, wherein a sizable chunk of land is not acquired, creates another phenomenon; when neither land is needed nor the labour.

6 Power, Politics, and Struggles over Land

It may be important to see the struggles over land and water on KHEP through the larger political problem of Kashmir's conflict. Yet doing so here, will, however, not do justice to the power asymmetry and agency of the poor at the grassroots level. Therefore, what is being stressed and mainly discussed in this chapter is the peasant's struggle against land-grabs. Even though there are different forms of resistance at play but all these struggles are mundane advocacy and lately open but non-violent in nature, which differentiates this struggle from the larger Kashmiri struggle. However, while putting major focus on the peasant resistance, here an attempt is made to understand the resistance provided by the external actors as well. This is done to understand how that resistance influences, shapes, affects, and strengthens or weakens the peasants' resistance against the land-grabs.

Scholarship on peasant resistance reflects, right from the times of Marx until the Chinese revolution, that peasantry was seen as a passive class. Marx famously described peasants as a 'sack of potatoes', as he was convinced that they are incapable of galvanizing themselves as a collective force as an agent of political change.[1] He therefore, was against passive resistance, specifically in the context of Prussia, by insisting passive resistance as a counter-revolutionary strategy of bourgeois (Hardiman 2013). However, as Hannah Arendt (1970) argues, that even though Marx was aware about the role of violence in the history, but this role, to him, was secondary; not violence as such. He regarded the State as an instrument of violence at the command of the ruling class; but the actual power of the ruling class did not consist of nor rely on violence. It was defined by the role the ruling class played in society, or more exactly, by its role in the process of production. It was Frantz Fanon, and more importantly Jean Paul Sartre, in preface of Fanon's book *The Wretched of the Earth*, who stretched further than Fanon, stating, 'Irrepressible violence ... is man recreating himself', that it is 'mad fury' through which 'the wretched of the earth' can 'become men' (Arendt 1970: 11–12).

Fanon, Sartre, and other western leftist intellectuals' arguments got an arm with the Chinese revolution in 1948, whereby Mao proclaimed, 'Power grows out of the barrel of a gun' and the rise of Vietnam and Cuban resistance and peasant movement, whereby peasants' demands were taken seriously, so as to avoid peasant revolutions and collective 'heroic' resistance movements, were celebrated (Wolf 1969).

However, over the years, these 'heroic' violent means of resistance were contested with some of the very important works on non-violent peasant resistance, which came from *Weapons of the Weak* by Scott (1985) and 'Everyday Politics in Peasant Societies' by Kerkvliet (2009). Both of these works argued that it is the unstructured, unorganized, covert, subtle, and mundane everyday resistance of peasants which is more effective than the structured collective resistance argued by the Marxists or the 'heroic' resistance argued by Wolf (1969). On the other hand; O'Brien and Li (2006) in their study on peasant resistance in China offer a very

---

[1] In *The Eighteenth Brumaire of Louis Bonaparte*, Marx famously referred to the Prussia Peasantry as a 'Sack of Potatoes' (1963–7).

interesting variant of Scott and Kerkvliet's work, which came to be known as 'rightful resistance'. They argue that peasants invoke the promises provided by the leaders and the constitutional laws to demand their rights through unstructured and unorganized resistance, but it is not covert, it is overt resistance. While everyday forms of resistance were observed as disguised, anonymous, quiet, and mundane; rightful resistance was described as more open, public, and noisy (O'Brien 2013). However, peasants' resistance against land in disputed territories or in conflict zones has a distinction from the land-grabs in other regions. For example, land-grabs, dispossession, and displacement is Israel's state policy in Palestine, therefore, peasants' fight is beyond material interests (Forman and Kedar 2004). Likewise, Peer and Ye (2015) argue that peasants in Kashmir fight against the land-grabs done by military, and every land-grab is connected with the larger 'occupation of the Kashmir'.

Numerous studies on contemporary land-grabs and resistance of peasants have majorly drawn from Marx (1976), Wolf (1969), Scott (1985), and Harvey (2003) (see Chapter 2). However, Tania Li's (2011) work 'Centering Labor in the Land Grab Debate', and Borras and Franco's (2013) work on 'Global Land Grabbing and Political Reactions "From below"', give us insight how land-grabs resistance is at play at different levels in various forms. Li argues peasant resistance in contemporary land-grabs is fought either to prevent land-grabs or to demand more compensation (Li 2011). Borras and Franco identified three important contestations around current land-grabbing: 'poor people versus corporate, poor people versus the State, and poor people versus poor people. While poor people versus corporate is a fight for remuneration, more compensation, employment, ecology, and so on; poor people versus the state is about expulsion, relocation, and resettlements. Poor people versus poor people is the fight inter and intra-class' (Borras and Franco 2013). However, in this context, as I discussed in the previous chapters and would further argue in this chapter, poor people versus poor people confrontation is not much visible, pervasive, and importantly, relevant. Therefore, I am adding another category: poor people versus village elites. Here I do not ditch the claim that there is no poor-poor contestation. It might exist, but as,

I have discussed in the last chapter and will further demonstrate that in this chapter, that it is the poor versus village elite/absentee landlords contestation which is pervasive here. With this background, I take a leaf from Scott (1985), Kerkvliet (2009), O'Brien and Li (2006), Li (2011), and Borras and Franco (2013) studies, coupled with conflict studies and resistance studies, such as the works of Randle (1994), Sundar (2007), Forman and Kedar (2004), Adnan (2011), and Baviskar (2008) to analyse the resistance to land-grabs in Kashmir.

The chapter then goes on to discuss the historical account of peasants' resistance in Badwan and Khopri. It gives a detailed account of how peasants responded to the land acquisition process. It further explains how people fought the lonely battle to stop the land-grabbing, whereby neither media nor the local administration or Kashmiri civil society supported them. This chapter further explains the transition from resistance against land-grabs to resistance for compensation. It talks about how people are caught in 'compensation trap' with the state authorities interestingly supporting them to get the political mileage out of it. The chapter shows the external dimension of resistance to KHEP, whereby this resistance comes from media, civil society, and Jammu and Kashmir. The chapter ends with concluding remarks on the entire discussion.

Lonely Battle: The Fight against Land-Grabs

In 1994 the Government of India envisioned to build Kishanganga HEP and officially informed Pakistan about its plan. The initial design of the HEP was about 75 metres in height, spread on 962.50 acres of land. This was to displace 25 villages constituting 961 families. However, the plan was faced with a strong resentment from some environmental groups and more importantly, external resistance from Pakistan, claiming that the HEP construction violates the IWT (for further details see section four of this chapter). While the deliberations about HEP construction were going on between the two countries, in 2000, an MoU was signed between the State government of Kashmir and Central government for the construction of KHEP. However, as noted in Chapter 4, those who were to be most affected—peasants—were not consulted or even informed. They came to know about the HEP construction in the year 2002, when the then Chief Minister of Kashmir, while addressing a rally in Gurez, announced the decision. A local peasant recalls what the Chief Minister said:

> He [the then chief minister of Kashmir] told us that he will give adequate compensation for our land and houses. While addressing people here, he said: We need to build a dam here to generate electricity. The HEP is for the national development. India will benefit from it, Kashmir will benefit from it and you the people will benefit from it. If you resist, we can use force to take the possession of the land and your house, better is we sort-out the issue amicably. (Author interview with peasant Asad Lone, Badwan 2011)

As the Chief Minister finished his talk, people in one voice raised objections about the HEP construction and stressed that they were completely against the KHEP. Reacting to peasants' objection, while leaving from the venue, the Chief Minister reiterated that the corporation would provide them enough compensation, but the people would be displaced and dispossessed—a cost people had to pay for 'national development'. The Chief Minister's statement made it clear that the State was determined not only to facilitate the land-grabs for capital, but was ready to walk an extra mile to control the land and houses arbitrarily, with the use of extra-economic force. However, Pakistan exerted its pressure on India to change the HEP design which coincided with resentment from the locals, and it forced India to modify the design of the HEP. As a result, in June 2006, India reduced the height of the HEP from 75 metres to 37 metres, which to a large extent addressed Pakistan's concerns. At the same time, displacement of only two villages and dispossession of further three villages from their lands was envisioned. With the design modification from the initial proposal of displacement of 25 villages, to the displacement of two villages, the pressure on the State and corporation against land-grabs started decreasing. What follows in this section is the process of resistance of villages Badwan and Khopri against the land-grabs.

With the modification in the HEP design, the two villages—Badwan and Khopri—which were earlier fighting the battle alongside other 23 villages against the HEP, found themselves lonely. As the population size of the would be affected area decreased, so did their importance, a common phenomenon in the contemporary land-grabs; where the size of affected—land and people—are seen as more important than the process, actors, and reasons (Edelman 2013). With the passage of time, nobody from the government or from the corporation came to them to talk about the HEP. Peasants had by now thought that the HEP construction plan has been shelved. But one fine morning in 2009, additional district commissioner of Bandipora came to Badwan, spent a few minutes, and informed the peasants that their land and houses have been acquired by the government for the HEP construction. This bombshell from the bureaucrat unnerved the peasantry, and pushed them to think of the memories of having and losing their homeland, but at the same time, these memories rejuvenated them to fight against the land and house-grabbing. Peasants initially began their struggle from 'advocacy politics' (Kerkvliet 2009), through a direct concerted effort by advocating their stand of having 'natural right' on their property and claiming to have a right to 'not-to move'. Besides advocacy politics, peasants further used 'rightful' and 'everyday forms of resistance' (O'Brien and Li 2006; Scott 1985) to raise their demands. People initially approached the corporation, local politicians, and sub-district and district administrative authorities. The corporation told them it is the State, which acquires the land, and the corporation has no role in land acquisition process. The local politicians gave them hopes that their grievances, would be taken to authorities and some amicable solution would be reached. However, the local administration told them categorically that politicians are fooling them (peasants) and giving them wrong hopes. Peasants were also informed that the land is for 'public purpose' therefore, no amount of resistance could stop the State from taking the land. Not assuaged by the bureaucratic dogma, that the resistance would yield no results, people continued to approach the bureaucracy and conveyed to them, their stand, of not giving them the land. However, they were told their land had been already acquired with the consent from village elites (see details in Chapter 5). As I have discussed in Chapter 4, in order to control the dissent, the State initially took the land of the elites—which they purposely decided to give first on rent, and later on permanently, so that the marginalized could not resist.

While imposing the doctrine of eminent domain, State could have taken the land anyway, with use of power, however, taking the land of elites made the land acquisition process much easier for the State. It was a move, where, once the big fish is caught; small ones will fall in the trap. Yet, when poor peasants resisted, the state arbitrarily controlled the land with use of extra-economic and extra-judicial coercion.

Living on the actual LoC, away from the galore of media and civil society, the peasants in Badwan and Khopri lost their battle against land-grabs, in which they got no external support. Here Michael Randle's (1994) two characteristics of 'civil resistance', that is, resistance as a collective action; and avoidance of 'any asymmetric recourse to violence' provides a good handle to understand peasant resistance in the context of Gurez. Randle argues, that in classical political theory, armed revolt is seen as an ultimate sanctity against the abuse of power. However, except in few weak states, armed revolt is not possible in the modern states, especially when huge military forces and weapons are at the disposal of these states. While the Indian Adivasi armed uprising against capital expansion somehow negates Randle's argument, nevertheless, it is important and relevant in the context of landlocked areas, such as Gurez. Here peasants, without any external support, could not afford to resort to resistance against the State, especially when the region is in military control. I have also stated in Chapter 3 that people's survival in Badwan and Khopri depends on maintaining a good relation with the military. Thus resistance of peasantry against land-grabs has to be situated within the context of Kashmiri conflict, and India's imagination of Kashmir being anti-national forces India to take measures at curbing any kind of unrest as necessary for national interest. The very dependence on military makes it impossible for the people to defy the 'rule of law' when the brute force is used and State defines what is 'legal and illegal protest'. This becomes complex when one type of 'resistance', for example, in case of British India whereby peaceful dissent was accepted but any kind of open resistance was dealt with harsh treatment (Hardiman 2013). Likewise, in Badwan and Khopri the peaceful resistance for compensation (which we shall discuss in the next section of this chapter) was allowed by the State. However, any kind of open resistance against land acquisition was categorically told to not be tolerated. Here, any kind of collective resistance, which state would assume can turn to violent or reach national and sub-national levels, was nipped in the bud with the use of brute force.

In India, the democratic setup paves the way for resisters to achieve their goals through peaceful protests (like in Singur, Narmada, and others) (Jones 2009). In Kashmir on the other hand, even the protests for water and electricity are seen as protests against the Indian state. Often mistaken for protests for independence of the state, these are thus dealt with an iron fist. The aggrieved protestors were from Uri—where NHPC runs two power projects. As part of negotiation to take their land for Uri HEPs, disposed peasants were promised round-the-clock free electricity after the HEP becomes operational. However, NHPC did not keep its promise. People would get less than eight hours of electricity in 24 hours. Therefore they resorted to protest against the corporation at the Uri receiving station. The security guards of the receiving station opened fire, thereby killing a youth from the area (Ishfaq-ul-Hassan 2012).

Within this background of absence of democratic space and execution of extrajudicial force by the state, to mussel the voices of those who fight for the rights, NHPC is seen an offshoot of the Indian State in Kashmir; therefore resistance against NHPC is equated to resisting the Indian state. And this, for the people of Badwan and Khopri, would yield no positive result; at least in the peasant's perspective.[2] This perception is more reinforced among village elders who feel helplessness in front of the corporation who—overtly or covertly— is supported by military and

---

[2] While Narmada, Nandigram, and others, are seen as major issues and covered by national newspapers and 24x7 news channels, the resistance in Kashmir is coloured with different angle. Not only does Indian army and government see Kashmir as 'other', Indian media and civil society, alike, also see it is a separate entity. Therefore treatment given to it is like the treatment given to a colony.

the state and hence expect and pray for external intervention to stop the work on KHEP. Subhan Mir, who I have spent time with, discussing local politics, NHPC work, land-grabs, and cross border infiltration in his agricultural field near the police station of Gurez, just one kilometre ahead of Daver market, explains this helplessness as, 'you can't fight the institutions—NHPC, state, and military—from whom you need a permission to breathe in this areas.' Mir feels the corporation's interest is 'national' development; they do not care what locals want:

> I have spent 60 years of my life here. I do not want to move from here. They say the HEP is for the development of the country ... so we have to sacrifice for the *development* of India. Who cares about what we want? We cannot fight against an Indian Corporation and the Indian government. They are powerful. I wish the people from the other side of the border [Pakistan] would attack this dam; otherwise, NHPC will not stop construction. (Author interview with a local peasant, Subhan Mir, June 2011. Emphasis in original conversation)

I finished discussion with Mir at around 4:30 p.m. and decided to return to my guesthouse in Daver before sunset—the time set by army for local people to return home. While walking back, I went to Daver market to buy some cookies and drinks, where I found two men in civvies following me. Initially I thought they were just going in the same direction where I was going. But they kept following me until I reached my guesthouse. In the evening, at the dinner table, I asked the gatekeeper of the guesthouse, if he has seen some people in civvies following me. He replied saying, 'They have been keeping track of your every movement'. Upon asking who they are, he replied, 'They are from IB [intelligence bureau]. They keep vigil on every outsider who comes here. You just noticed it. Others do not'.

Helplessness of people like Mir has to be seen within the conditions under which these people live, where people cannot even breathe without the military's permission. Nonetheless, foyer politics, gossiping, and evening discussions in kitchens are what Scott (1985) described as 'weapons of the weak' here. However, a university student of Gurez, who I met in his home in Badwan, sees the issue at macro-level and argues that land-grabs in Badwan and Khopri cannot win unless Kashmir dispute is resolved. He feels they are very much a part of this Kashmiri struggle and the corporation also treats them like Kashmiri militants or sympathizers of the movement; therefore, they more hostile attitude towards people in Gurez, as their voices are not heard outside:

> Unless Kashmir dispute is not solved, we will face economic, social and political problems here. India wants to exploit our Natural resources through NHPC. Its sole purpose is to control our land and resources through force. What British did to India during colonization period, India is doing to us. [He sobs!] (Author interview with a Kashmir University student from Gurez, June 2013)

Examining why peasants could not succeed in stopping land acquisition, it comes out that (a) the absentee land lords gave up their lands first, which made it easy for the State to muscle the poor, (b) the existence of doctrine of eminent domain, whereby under the Land Acquisition Act 1984, the State can forcibly take any land for 'public purpose', (c) the absence of a democratic space in the state, where every protest is seen as a protest against India, therefore dealt harshly with by police and military forces, and (d) lastly the resistance offered by the peasants went unrecognized and unreported due to the landlocked nature of the area, which remains, most of the times, out of the purview of media and researchers; who can report the cases of abuse. Besides the obnoxious land acquisition Act, the absence of democratic space and the failure on the part of peasants to mobilize and galvanize the outside public, political, and media support (some of the key elements argued by Borras and Franco (2013) as a recipe for succeeding in political struggles) led peasants to believe in the futility of resistance. As the peasants lose the battle of land-grabbing, they turned to be what Popkin (1979: 18) described as primarily self-interested political actors, who make rational choices to advance their individual interests, therefore, in the absence of any alternative, they started battling for enough compensation; though not just for economic wellbeing as Popkin argues. We shall discuss the resistance for compensation in the next section.

The Resistance for Compensation and the Support from 'Messiahs'

Losing the battle against land-grabs, peasant resistance made a transition from resistance against dispossession and displacement to resistance for compensation. However, quite surprisingly, with this transition, local politicians started to take part in this movement for 'enough compensation'. While normally people of the area living under the shadow of a gun and away from the eyes of the State machinery, are not in a position to lead open protest, however, this time they could manage to break the silence and started a resistance movement, as they got support from an unexpected quarter when the local lawmaker not only joined the peasants' resistance but also mobilized peasants to lead protests against the corporation for 'enough compensation'. For peasants like Mir this was quite surprising, as initially the MLA was indifferent when they would discuss with him about the land-grabs. But as soon as the land was taken, the whole struggle got confined to demanding adequate compensation. Mir Sahab said, that the MLA sahib told him:

> I am with you; the government is with you. We should fight for the compensation. The company should give us enough compensation. It took our land; it exploited our natural resources, so it should provide employment, houses and compensation of our houses. (Author interview with a peasant from Badwan, May 2011)

Nevertheless, the very support of the local lawmaker encouraged the peasants to lead an open protest. But the support of the lawmaker and the approval, not oppression by the state, to allow or to be part of the resistance was regarded by some peasants as a mere tactic by the lawmaker to gain political legitimacy by playing the 'victim card'.[3] A social activist of the region stated:

> Local legislator and the government he represents are equally responsible for land-grabs. In fact, the local government is the main party, which

[3] Local politicians as well as the local government play the victim card that they are helpless in front of the corporation, which is a Government of India entity.

facilitated land-grabs. Local leaders are exploiting the poor peasants. First, they did not show any sympathy to peasants while taking their land and houses, but now as they have got control over land, they offer them false promises of adequate compensation. The corporation has got what it wants—land and waters. Even if it pays now more money as compensation, it would not matter much for such a big corporation. (Author interview with a social activist, based in Srinagar, June 2013)

Within this realm of resistance for compensation peasants had now found a 'messiah' in the form of the local lawmaker. However, subsistence farmers and economically underprivileged people like Ganais still feel that their voices were not being heard; no matter how loud they were. They believed, they were not being given a chance to speak to HCC and government officers by the village elites, and no government official, politician, or even media listened to them whenever they visited the villages. A peasant Khadija Baigum narrated:

We do not want to be displaced, we love our homeland. Our ancestors are buried here. We need to come to offer prayers for them. How can we come here again? Those bade log [elites] who decided on our behalf, are actually responsible for our miseries. They say project is for the National development ... but what about our development? (Author interview with Khadija Baigum, a peasant, July 2012)

People like Khadija have not seen the NHPC people and have never talked to anyone of them. For her it is the local elites who are responsible for her woes, a clear sign of poor-elite contestation. Everyday resistance of these people goes beyond the fight for compensation or against dispossession; rather it has more to do with their sway in decision-making at the local level. While on the one hand the issues of 'local development versus national development' are core of the narratives here, whereby the 'former' is neglected for the betterment of 'latter' (Zulu and Wilson 2012), peasants in Badwan and Khopri find snatching of their resources or what Scott (1985) calls 'material interests' more important than Kashmiris' demand of equal rights under IWT. Nevertheless, resources abundance in the form of fresh water resources for hydroelectric generation are categorized as so called 'resource curse' (Sachs and Warner 1997) for whole of Kashmir, including Gurez:

> NHPC wants to illuminate Hindustan [India]. Neither Gurez or Bandipora nor Kashmir gets benefit of it. We are helpless; we cannot do anything against NHPC or Indian state. Just we have to accept the fact that we have to leave from here. (Author interview with a local peasant, Khalil Lone, July 2012)

Within this dynamic of narratives of exploitation by the capital and the State, foyer politics in the village is vibrant. People often gather on the banks of a trout stream, near a bridge, outside a mosque, and outside a small barbershop to discuss issues arising from HEP construction. Corruption and nepotism by the government officials by favouring elites and neglecting the poor is the favourite topic. Everyday forms of resistance, such as gossiping, backbiting, and abusing government officials for changing land records to give unfair support to the corporation, are dominant narratives in any formal and informal discussion. A peasant and local political leader has this account to offer:

> There is a complete nexus between the government officers and the NHPC employees. The Tehsildar [sub-divisional magistrate] gets blankets, oil, spices besides bribes from the corporation. So does a revenue clerk from a nearby village. These government officers in turn change the land records to show agriculture land as barren land to help the corporation. If the poor peasant goes to meet them, he/she can never find them ... but they are always available for NHPC people. NHPC rewards them with cash and kind, what will they get from us ... poor people? So they change our land records to show it as a government land or forestland, to help the corporation. (Author interview with a peasant and a local politician, May 2012)

Likewise, M.Y. Lone, who also works for HCC, says his land records were changed by the local officials to help the corporation:

> The revenue department people here temper the land records. I have 21 kanals of land but on the revenue records they are showing only

1 kanal. I have to go to pillar to post everyday to explain the land records situation here. Most of the people here are uneducated. Land was not demarcated before the NHPC started building dam. All of us knew our land as our ancestors had demarcated it for us. Now as they have taken this land, they declare it as a state land. But we know it is our ancestral land. We will fight for it.

The state-corporate nexus is seen as one of the main roadblock for the peasants to succeed in their resistance. Peasants believe land record clerks, divisional magistrate and other governments officers take dolls from HCC and NHPC, and in return help them to control the dissent. They also change land records. In some cases people cannot get papers of their private land, as that has been declared as state land on papers.

Nevertheless, as it has happened to many peasant resistant movements, the movement here seems not to be yielding any positive result. In the absence of NHPC's adequate response to the complaints of peasants from Badwan and Khopri, in June 2012, the *Sarpanch*, asked the peasants, including HCC employees of the twin villages, to stop/block the work on HEP construction. This strike, or what locals call *Karo ya maro tehreekh* (Do or Die Movement), has been launched to demand fulfilment of the promises which the corporation has made to the peasants. Naseer Ganai, a peasant from Khopri who works with HCC, says they had no choice but to stage a movement against the corporation that has been exploiting them:

> We have started this *Tehreek* [movement], therefore, I did not go to work, and so did not other people who work in HCC. Unless they meet our demands, we will not call off our strike. We are around 20 employees from this village who work with the HCC, besides us, there are hundreds of other people who work in the project, but all of them are outsiders, from India. (Author interview with a peasant and HCC Employee, Bashir Ganai, June 2012)

For two days nobody from HCC or government visited the protesters. It seems the suspension of work did not bother them. However, the Sarpanch believes that, their resistance would force the corporation and government to come and listen to them. I met Mr Chuhan and asked him why HCC is not paying the peasants enough compensation, he replied by saying, 'peasants are exploiting the Corporation. They do not want to work'. He explained to me, 'We give them money, education scholarships to their children, house in Srinagar or Bandipora, besides that we are planning to build infrastructure here. What else do they want?'

The June 2012 open protest is a part of the long resistance by the peasants against the HCC to meet their demands of house construction, employment and so on. Prior to the June protests, peasants have staged a series of open protests against the HCC for not fulfilling its promises. In July 2011, protesters led by a lawmaker and a local assembly member halted the work of HCC until the company fulfilled the promises of employment, which it had made to the local people in 2009 (Rasool 2011).

Similarly, in 2010, peasants protested and stopped the work of HCC because the company had so far failed to provide employment to the local people. A peasant and Indian Congress party worker who spearheaded the protests described the NHPC as an exploitative agency, which displaces people by developing dams. He narrated:

> We will not call off strike; we will not allow them to work on dam, unless the NHPC and government give us final commitment to build our houses and provide employment till September 2012. (Author interview with Majnoon Lone, a peasant and political worker, July 2012)

As September 2012 has passed, however, most of the demands of the peasants are yet to be met. The resistance movement so far has bothered neither the corporation nor the government. Therefore, people are left with few options. To the politicians they do not matter much, as their number is small and taking legal action is too expensive for them. Abdullah Mir says that peasants cannot afford to fight the case against the corporation in court, and their protests are not yielding any results either:

> Majority of the people here are poor. We have a court of sub judicial magistrate here, but that court does not have the authority to issue order/ stay in such a high profile case like HEP. If we have to file a case against

the corporation, we need to go to the High Court in Srinagar or Supreme Court in Delhi. But both these courts are inaccessible for us, not because we are prohibited, but our socio-economic condition does not allow us to do so. (Author interview with a peasant, Abdullah Mir, September 2012)

While the courts are too far and too expensive for the poor people to afford, which has been even accepted by the Supreme Court of India (*Tribune* 2013),[4] the district administration is equally alien to these people. To reach the District Administrator's office, they need to go to Bandipora. Getting to Bandipora takes them one full day. With no frequent transport available, high-engine vehicles ferry passengers and charge each passenger 600 rupees (USD 12) roundtrip, which is roughly equal to the amount of money for which a five-member family can feed itself for a month. This is unaffordable for poor peasants like Ganais. Under these circumstances, it is the local well-to-do people or members of the village middle class who go to the district headquarters to plead the case of the peasants. A retired forest officer and a local political worker of the area narrated:

I had three meetings with District Commissioner [DC]. I told him; I am just knocking your door every time that people are suffering. I told DC, tell them NHPC make the dam, and then throw us into the dam ... because you do not understand our demands. (Author interview with Asad lone, Badwan, August 2012)

In the middle of this helplessness, people are left to accept the state order, as a peasant narrates; 'I am a poor man how could I resist. And when we see the elite people are happy and take decision to leave their homes, what can we poor people do?'

---

[4] Highlighting, the fact that litigation has become expensive in India, a division bench of Supreme Court of India on 25 August, 2013 observed: 'In the present era, the legal profession, once known as a noble profession, has been converted into a commercial undertaking. Litigation has become so expensive that it has gone beyond the reach and means of a poor man' (*Tribune* 2013).

While the class and caste contestation does come out in conversations, but there is contestation of the means and ways of resistance among the age group and sex as well. For example, women in Badwan and Khopri do not come in the open to protest. But their resistance is often a daily and covert expression. Apart from discussing it among themselves and blaming the corporation for exploitation, some of them come out in the open to talk about it with anyone who visits their home. They also persuade male members of their family to visit government and corporate offices to fight for their rights. On the other hand, men are using everyday, overt, covert, and 'intermediate' (Turton 1986: 36) forms of resistance or sometimes taking defiant confrontation with the company by stopping its work and speaking against the government. Likewise, young students who study outside Gurez speak more openly against the corporation and government. So do educated people who use media to communicate their resistance. Mohammad Amin Lone, a retired officer, who I have spent good time with, discussing the issues in Gurez, gave me a letter which he wanted me to get published in a local newspaper in Srinagar. Since postal service here was not so regular and people do not have much access to newspapers, Amin thought that sending this letter through me would ensure it reaches to the newspaper office in time (see Figure 6.1). The letter reads:

KHEP that is being built in a beautiful village called Badwan. The dam construction has adversely affected the ecology in Badwan. Trees were also cut down and the projects have affected agriculture and grazing areas that are of immense importance for this village. Control on grazing lands has also affected livestock. Government should take immediate steps to prevent the outbreak of diseases in the areas such as Badwan, Wanpora, Matrigam, Kralpora etc that are being affected by the construction of dam, so that to prevent people to get sick. Government should also take immediate steps to rehabilitate people and provide them adequate compensation, jobs in government and construct houses for them.

Thus the peasants use 'circumstance based resistance', wherein the forms of resistance change in the context of the environment they live in.

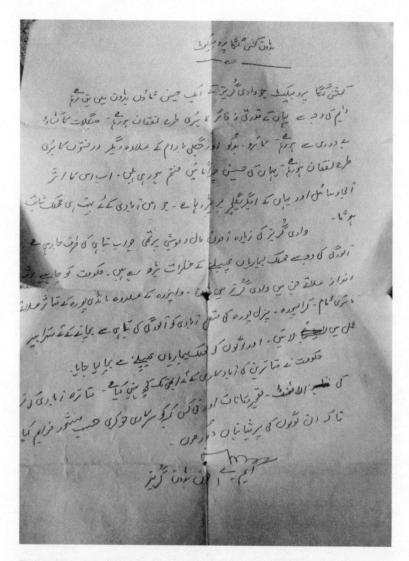

Figure 6.1 Letter Written by M. Amin Lone to a Newspaper for Publication. The Letter is Addressed to the Government to Take Note of the Problems Faced by People of Gurez due to HEP
Source: Author.

Whatever be the form of resistance, state's indifferent attitude towards protecting the rights of the local people is visible. However, people's resistance against land-grabs or for 'adequate' compensation continues. While resistance against land-grabs is not an option now, resistance for 'enough compensation' is the only potent weapon of the peasants to make the state and corporation to give up the land. Poor people's resistance for more compensation is actually a resistance against the land-grabs. A peasant stated:

> In the situation where nobody is with you, neither the State, nor the media or civil society ... we lost our land. When they took our land forcibly, we had no option left, but to ask for more compensation. We want them to give us as *enough* compensation, if they cannot give, then they should stop the work here and return us our land. (Author interview with a peasant in Khopri, June 2013. Emphasis in original conversation)

This kind of resistance for compensation might be bracketed as everyday political strategy of risk aversion by the poor as they have already lost the rights on their land. In this process, peasants are either self-interested political actors who make rational choice to averse the risks (Popkin 1979) or they fall in what is known as 'compensation trap' (Van Rooij et al. 2012) whereby, the corporation increases or promises to giving more compensation, whenever the peasants protest.

Whilst the peasants struggle against land-grabs and for 'enough compensation', the state and civil society of Kashmir has also been actively resisting the KHEP and are demanding adequate compensation for the peasants and the state of Jammu and Kashmir. Frequent newspaper reports/articles (see for example, Jaleel 2005; Maqbool 2011; Rasool 2011) from Kashmir, have criticized HEP construction on the basis of its fallout on the ecology and displacement of the Dard-Shina tribe. Likewise, local politicians such as the Deputy Speaker of Jammu and Kashmir legislative assembly, which signed the deal with the corporation, have also now become critical of the corporation for not committing to the promises and destroying the ecology. For example, in July 2011, the former Chief Minister of Kashmir and the son of the ex-Chief Minister, who facilitated land-grabs, during his visit to Gurez, castigated the corporation for not fulfilling the promise it had made to the peasants, and at the same time he raised serious concerns about ecological destruction caused by the corporation (Rasool 2011). Besides former minister, there are several other politicians such as the Minister of Irrigation, lawmaker and minister from Gurez, lawmaker from Communist Party of India, and separatists who have been critical of NHPC on KHEP. While some like the former Chief Minister, Minister of Irrigation and Law maker of Gurez, and Lawmaker of Langate called NHPC the British East India Company—for exploiting Kashmir's resources. Others like separatist leader, Gilaani, see land-grabbing and control on resources through NHPC as a part of India's 'imperial design' to control the region.[5]

State and Civil Society's Fight for Compensation

The resistance for 'adequate' compensation for the power projects, water usage, and land-grabs came soon after the central government did not agree to construct the Dulhasti power project—the second HEP in the state, on the same lines of the first HEP—Salal—which allowed the state to buy back the project at depreciated cost, in accordance with Kashmir Electricity Supply Act, 1971. According to the Act, half of the power generated from the HEPs constructed by NHPC would be made available for the state at generation cost, while the profits from the rest of the 50 per cent power would be shared between the state and the centre equally. Moreover, the state would have sole rights of developing fisheries and navigation in the reservoir created by the project. While the terms were accepted verbally, the central government did not put them in writing (CSC 2011: 6). In 1980, NHPC prepared to build the Dulhasti HEP, however, not on the same conditions of Salal, but on the conditions of fixing of percentage of power. That is to say, 15 per cent of the generating capacity would be kept 'unallocated' at the disposal of the central government, and 85 per cent of the remaining electricity would be distributed among the states. The home state (Kashmir) would be given 1.5 paisa per unit for the energy generated by the power station.

---

[5] Author interview with Syed Ali Shah Gilaani, July 2012.

Moreover, the project would be undertaken directly by NHPC. This change of position by NHPC from the earlier agreement upset the then Chief Minister, who wrote a direct letter to the then Union Energy Minister on 16 January 1981, that these power sharing agreements 'would deprive the state from yielding benefits of its natural endowment'. This was the first attempt on the part of Kashmir government to fight for its rights. Thus marked the beginning of resistance against the NHPC, and the resistance for equal share for its waters, which the state believes it had been deprived of under the IWT.

Since then every Chief Minister of the state has raised the issue of exploitation of the state's water resources and demanded adequate compensation for it. However, at the local level, many people see it as a mere political gimmick rather than a genuine desire of politicians to get back these projects. These projects are taking place in the upper mountain areas of Kashmir, which are apt for hydroelectric generation, but remain landlocked most of the time due to heavy snowfall and the absence of proper road and rail communication, which limits the social mobility of people; therefore the social and ecological costs of the HEPs did not become a public debate. Moreover, the absence of independent media, and the very subsidy culture injected by India in the form of subsidies for food, kerosene oil, gas, and providing government jobs to 'win the hearts' of Kashmir to become 'truly' Indian, the economic and social issues did not become a concern for the larger Kashmiri community. This trend continued till the armed insurgency against Indian rule in Kashmir broke out in 1989.

From 1989, Kashmir witnessed a serious bloody conflict, which cost thousands of Kashmiri lives. Therefore neither NHPC nor the economic woes, or natural resources exploitation became a debate. Here the fight was for liberation of the whole of Kashmir's land, not the 'relatively small' portion of land or water resources under the control of NHPC, which the resistance leaders claimed would automatically, come under the state's control when Kashmir would gain an independent status. However, with the use of military force, India was able to bring relative normalcy to the region by early 2000. The return of 'normalcy', however, marked the second phase of resistance against NHPC and its exploitation of resources. On 7 October 2004, the then Chief Minister of the state wrote a letter to the

Prime Minister of India, Manmohan Singh, that the state had not been compensated for its water resources but exploited on account of the IWT. He demanded that Salal 690 MW HEP be returned to the state. While the Indian Prime Minister responded on 13 October 2004 with a note that he received the letter about the transfer of power project, he did not promise to return the project, nor was the project transferred back to the state (CSC report 2011). On the contrary, the Power Minister of India expressed strong reservations about return of the power project based on the adverse commercial impacts on NHPC and the lack of expertise in the state to run these HEPs.

However, with the resistance against exploitation of Kashmiri resources rising, the Prime Minister of India constituted five working groups to look into different aspects of problems faced by the state and the means to address them. One of the groups on economic development of Kashmir, headed by C. Rangrajan, Chairman of the Indian Prime Minister's Economic Advisory Council, strongly recommended that the Salal HEP be returned to the state to partially compensate it for the discrimination it faced due to the IWT. However, after opposition by the Power Ministry of India, the report changed its recommendation of transferring Salal to transferring Dulhasti HEP. However, none of the recommendations has been met so far.

Since the present Chief Minister took the reigns of the state, he has been vehemently demanding the return of power projects back to the state. Meanwhile, the separatists, who until the recent past would find it blasphemous to talk about the economic affairs have been criticizing the NHPC for exploiting Kashmiri resources. Separatist leader Syed Ali Shah Geelani puts it in this way:

> There is a full control of military here. Actually India wants to control all our natural resources. NHPC employs outside people, cuts forest trees and destroys environment here. The electricity is produced for the people of India, in Kashmir we have become sufferers.

On the other hand, voices outside the government against the NHPC have become louder. A group consisting of scholars, journalists, trade union leaders, and civil rights activists created a platform under the banner Kashmir Centre for Social and Development Studies (KCSDS). The civil society group headed by a traders' leader and an academician has been fighting and raising awareness about resource exploitation by NHPC. The group filed a case against NHPC in a local court and led to dozens of protests; and its members have led media campaigns through a series of articles published in the local newspaper about the NHPC. Some of the published articles are: 'Mini-Ratna NHPC an unfair player in JK power play' and 'NHPC Monopoly'. One newspaper article, titled 'The dubious role of NHPC in J&K' states:

> 76% of the total assets of NHPC are located in J&K while its generation in J&K is only around 24 percent of total generation. Has it come here to occupy our land instead of doing some serious business? (Zargar 2011)

The role of NHPC in water resources exploitation often makes news in local English and vernacular dailies.

Quite a reflection of local sentiment, Figure 6.2 depicts how NHPC is extracting electricity and resource from Kashmir and taking it to mainland

Figure 6.2   Cartoon Depicting NHPC Extracting Resources from Kashmir but Illuminating India
Source: Suhail Naqashbandi.

India. With mounting pressure from the local civil society, Kashmir based political parties have been making it a poll agenda to get the power projects back from Indian state, compensation and fair share in IWT.

In June 2011, the Government of Kashmir under pressure, formed a five-member committee of cabinet ministers to look into the issues arising from agreements on power projects with NHPC in the state. The 183-page report, including Annexure, which was accepted by the state cabinet, recommended that the state government should get the Salal project back at the depreciated costs based on the agreement, and the state should further take immediate action to get 47 per cent power from the Salal project against the allocated 35 per cent. The centre should also compensate for the losses due to the power share given to the state for only 35 per cent and not 47 per cent, as agreed in the MoU.

Furthermore, the report blames NHPC for using corruptive methods to make deals, and of stealing and hiding the agreement records. During the investigation, the committee found that the MoU papers of Salal HEP, the first HEP executed by NHPC in Kashmir, which was to become the basis of construction for the future HEPs, were missing from the state power development office, governor's office, and other offices. It was later proved that the file was purposely stolen by NHPC through some blue-eyed bureaucrats who were promised a bigger job in NHPC, quite akin to what Olivier De Schutter (2011) observed, that some government elites receive bribes or other concessions from the investors to cede the land away. Here it is not only the land but also the control on waters, and the land vis-à-vis the local state's sovereignty which has been compromised in lieu of corruption. Within this background, the report argues that the agreement of the state with the NHPC has been 'funding execution and operation', therefore ownership lies with the state and the projects should be bought back at depreciated costs. It further recommends that if the agency does not return the power projects, the state 'should forcefully seek transfer of Dulhasti' projects from NHPC.

Within this dynamic of the impact of NHPC projects and resistance against the same, the state assembly constituted a committee of lawmakers to look into the issues of ecological impacts due to the Kishanganga project. The committee suggested that the corporation has destroyed ecology during the tunnelling process. The head of the committee, M. Yousuf Tarigami, stated, 'Environmental norms have been violated by the corporation. There seems to be a huge destruction of ecology, and impact of our forest cover'.

In the midst of a power crisis in the valley, with many areas observing 10 hours of power curtailment daily, government is coming under heavy pressure from civil society actors to address the power deficit by bringing back power projects from NHPC. On 11 January 2017, the deputy Chief Minister and Power Minister of the state made a statement in Jammu and Kashmir Assembly, that the government has taken the issue of transfer of power projects with the central government, and they expect some break-through very soon. However, that seems unlikely to happen, as the state government is at a lack of will and courage to fight with the centre to get back these power projects. The absence of popular mandate and support for mainstream parties in the region is the reason they lake autonomy and capacity, which Fox (1993) sees as the two dimensions of state power—to be able to negotiate with the centre. Under those circumstances state resistance is nothing beyond lip service.

***

Peasants' struggles against the 'capital' in Badwan and Khopri, are often engulfed by larger narratives of two countries—India and Pakistan, about KHEP, which leads to submersion of the peasant narrative, which inter-estingly are the most affected actors of this HEP. People's resistance and Pakistan's pressure made India to change the HEP design and therefore decrease the adverse impact of the HEP from the initial plan of displac-ing twenty five villages to two villages. The two villages that were left out resisted the land-grabs and displacement but could not succeed in front of the mighty state which acquired their land and houses. As the peasants lost the battle against land-grabs, there was gradual transition in the nature of peasant resistance from resistance against land-grabs to the resistance for compensation, due to the realization among peasants that resistance for compensation and not resistance against the land-grabs is possible under the existing land acquisition law, and in the absence of democratic space in the region.

To quell peasant resistance at the ground level, the corporation increased or at least made promises to increase compensation. And compensation is just a tool used by the corporation to suppress the resistance against land-grabs in Kashmir. Where there is resistance against the projects, compensation is increased. Compensation in the form of cash, scholarships, and jobs, and so on are used as tools to make people agree to give up their land. While some peasants, mostly elders and women, fight against the dispossession and displacement, the State of Kashmir and the civil society, fight for compensation. The resistance for 'enough' compensation, however, is a peasant's strategy to demand and fight for the compensation which is beyond the control/capacity of the corporation. Since peasants cannot refuse the land to the state that is to be acquired for the 'public purpose' thus demanding more compensation is actually to annoy the state to give up the land. Yet the dichotomy of some people not resisting against the land and water grabs, has to do with inaccessibility of this area, which remains cut off for half of the year, due to heavy snowfall.

It is this very dependence on military, state, and exclusion from rest of the Kashmir population where these people have to offer resistance ... thus it is important to address what Kerkvliet (2009) points out understanding the resistance through political structure in which the resistance occurs. And, politics, as elaborated by him is about 'control, allocation, production and use of resources and values and ideas underlying those resources' (Kerkvliet 2009). Poor peasant's resistance here thus remains visible only in their own vicinity, as the district administration and higher judiciary is too far and too alien, and therefore too expensive to these people.

7 *Exploitation and Politics of Decision-Making*

After providing a detailed account of land-grabs around the world, actors involved in grabs, land-grabs in India, resistance to land-grabs, land tenure changes in Kashmir, development-induced dispossession in Badwan and Khopri villages (Bandipora district), and resistance offered by the people to these land-grabs, this chapter provides insights into the class dynamics of the land-grabbing process. To understand and analyse these complexities, this book, by using Henry's framework, raises four important questions about agrarian political economy concerning social relations of production and reproduction. These are: (*a*) Who owns what? (*b*) Who does what? (*c*) Who gets what?, and (*d*) What do they do with it? Bernstein (2010) argues that these four questions can be applied to different sites and scales of economic activity. The first question, 'Who owns what?' gives an understanding of how the means of production and re-production are distributed. The second question, 'Who does what?' is aimed to understand the social divisions of labour. The third question, 'Who gets what?' inquires into the distribution of 'fruits of labour'. Finally, the fourth question, 'What do they do with it?' looks at how the distribution and use of social product is determined by different social relations of production and reproduction. These questions, though are critical for understanding class dynamics in rural settings, the analysis of land politics would be incomplete without understanding the question of decision making in land-grabs in disputed territories, such as Kashmir. Building on field experiences in Badwan and Khopri villages, this chapter raises one more critical question, 'Who gets to decide?', to analyse and understand power dynamics of land-grabs in Kashmir. The chapter provides a detailed account of the existing assets held by peasants, J&K state, and NHPC; the current livelihoods and projects they are engaged in; and the profits they earn from their existing works and how they use the capital generated from the means of production. Thus, this chapter is divided into sections in terms of questions of ownerships, division of labour, fruits of labour, and the utilization of the product—profits.

The Question of Ownership

The question of ownership, in tribal societies such as Gurez, is very complex. As illustrated in Chapters 4 and 5, peasants in Badwan and Khopri villages own modest houses, arable and non-arable land, as well as livestock in the form of horses, cattle, sheep, and cows. Peasants also have common property resources in the form of customary land, state land, and forest-land. All these resources were the primary means of production until the arrival of capital. When modern capital from NHPC ventured into the area, the means of production changed. Common property resources— water, forest, and grazing areas became the first casualty of capital, followed by private lands and residential houses. Even though the houses and the notified land is still in possession of the people, but the fact is, that land has been acquired by the State. What people are left with now, is a portion of their agricultural land without any formal rights over it, a compensation amount for their property, and a verbal promise from the State and the corporation that they will get a house in Bandipora or Srinagar.

According to NHPC, the corporation is in possession of 450.26 hectares of land in the region. However, just in the KHEP, NHPC has 'grabbed' 379.07 hectares of land.[1] Like KHEP, NHPC is running many other smaller or bigger HEPs in Kashmir. Huge swaths of land are taken for the construction of dams, colonies for the employees, power stations and so on, which suggest that the NHPC and the state land records heavily underestimate NHPC land holdings in the region. Besides land, the corporation is in control of seven HEPs in Kashmir. With a cumulative installed capacity of 2009 MW (recent figures after commissioning Uri-II), NHPC is currently constructing five other HEPs including the KHEP.

The State of Jammu and Kashmir on the other hand, owns a few small HEPs; although it has a *de facto* and *de jure ownership* of forests, state land, and water bodies. In this case, however, IWT curtails that right of the state to utilize the full potential of its water resources.

The Division of Labour

In the villages of Badwan and Khopri people are mainly engaged in farming. While men and women use farming as a fulltime job, children offer helping hand in harvesting. However, quite akin to hilly communities all over the world, peasants in this mountainous area are engaged in multiple livelihoods, due to their small or marginal landholdings. These off-farm livelihoods include, but are not limited to, raising livestock, running a small grocery, government employment, and daily wage labour with the military. As the corporation started the construction of dam, some peasants also got the employment with the corporation, albeit temporary. See Table 7.1 for main occupations of rural households in Gurez. Also see detailed illustration about division of labour in Chapter 4.

---

[1] The data was obtained from NHPC on 20 June 2013, under Right to information Act 2009.

Table 7.1   Main Occupations of Rural Households in Gurez

Occupation	No.	%
Student	1.4	18.9
Dependant	0.8	11.3
Farming	3.1	41.5
Labour	0.7	9.4
Service	1.4	18.9
Total	7.4	100.0

Source: Shabir et al. (nd).

Since its inception in 1975, NHPC has been engaged in HEP construction in Kashmir. The corporation is presently constructing nine power projects all over India, out of which five are being constructed in Kashmir, which includes KHEP. Moreover, NHPC is doing a survey for 1200 MW power project at Bursar in Kashmir, and is awaiting clearance from the central cabinet for the construction of three more projects.

The State of Jammu and Kashmir ironically plays just a brokers role. Its role in these land transactions has remained as a facilitator of the land deals. While the State on the one hand facilitates land-grabs, on the other hand it has strategically positioned itself against the NHPC to show resonance with the local demands and resistance against the NHPC's exploitation of water resources. The State in general identifies, facilitates, legalizes, controls and then transfers the land to the NHPC.

The Fruits of Labour

As ownership and division of labour changed with the arrival of capital, so did the outcomes of labour. It would not be out of place to stretch back, and briefly illustrate the situation before the arrival of capital. Peasants in the twin villages were producers as well as consumers of their own produce. Out of the average 10 kanals of farmland, they would harvest an average of four quintals of pulses, two to three quintals of wheat, besides vegetables for daily consumption. The livestock in the form of sheep, cows, and horses would also fetch them a sizable amount of income (see Table 7.2). Besides, the income from private property resources, the peasants would get a significant share of their income from edible wild vegetables and other forest products, firewood, grazing cattle in the pasture areas, condiments grown in the forests, and other medicinal plants. Those who were employed in government jobs would get an additional amount of 8,000 to 10,000 rupees on an average (around USD 150 or 160).

However, as the construction of KHEP has led to dispossession of private and common property resources, the peasants would no longer be able to reap the fruits of their labour—they have lost all these traditional livelihood options. As the corporation took control of their land and allied resources; it offered them a compensation amount of 600,000 rupees per kanal of land; besides a temporary job in the dam

Table 7.2   Livestock in Gurez

S. No.	Particulars	Number/ Quantity	Density/ sq.km
1.	Cattle population	8,500 (11)	23.40
2.	Breedable cattle	5,000	13.77
3.	Yak population	4,694 (6)	12.90
4.	Horse/mule population	3,704 (5)	10.20
5.	Sheep total	50,690 (66)	139.60
6.	Sheep cross-bred	28,243 (37)	77.88
7.	Sheep local	22,447 (29)	61.80
8.	Goat	9,054 (12)	24.90
9.	Wool production (kg)	79,076	–
10.	Mutton production (kg)	2,93,343	–
11.	Milk availability per capita (g/day)	136	–
12.	Average dairy milk yield per cow (L)	2.30	–
13.	No. of livestock per hectare of area sown	71.6	–
14.	Pasture and grazing lands to total reported area (%)	19.0	–

Source: District Livestock Census 2011–12. Department of Animal Husbandry. Government of Jammu and Kashmir.

construction site, against the monthly salary of eight to ten thousand rupees. The corporation agreed to provide them a house in the outskirts of the Srinagar city or in Bandipora district, the promise that has proved a hoax now.

Right from its inception in Kashmir, NHPC has got the lion's share from the HEPs run by it in the State. The corporation that was established with an initial investment of 2,000 million rupees has over the years transformed from a small enterprise to one of the top 10 PSUs in India with an investment base of 3,877,180 million rupees in 2010. NHPC in its yearly financial report of 2010–11 showed the net sale of 4,046 crore rupees (USD 797.516 million) and a profit of 2,166.67 crore rupees (USD 426.945 million). An RTI query in 2016, by the Commonwealth Human Rights Initiative (CHRI), to Union Ministry of Power/NHPC seeking information about transactions between the central Government of India and Government of Jammu and Kashmir revealed that the corporation has earned over 194 billion rupees from the power projects it runs in Kashmir from 2001 to 2015. During the same period NHPC sold 20, 841, 65 million units of power to J&K state alone, thus earning over 41 billion rupees. Interestingly, 40 per cent of the total electricity generated by NHPC in India comes from J&K (Yaseen 2016). While the NHPC is enjoying large-scale growth, on the contrary Kashmir has been losing its resources, against the 12 per cent royalty it gets for its land and water resources (see Figure 7.1).

Out of the three resources needed for the generation of electricity—land, water, and capital—Kashmir provides two resources, land and water, to NHPC. Professor Nisar Ali, the former economic advisor to Jammu

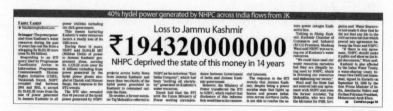

Figure 7.1 NHPC Power Generation in J&K
Source: Yaseen Faisul.

and Kashmir government, stated in an interview with this author that 'Kashmir has been exploited by NHPC'. The energy and finance starved state has to buy back electricity from the same company during winter seasons, at three times more cost than what it sells to the outside states. As per the MoUs signed between the State and the corporation, for the construction and implementation of the HEPs, the corporation is supposed to return the HEPs after a stipulated time, however so far no HEP was returned to the State (CSC 2011).

The Utilization of the Product

Peasants in Badwan and Khopri villages are largely engaged in subsistence farming; however, they do have surplus food grains, which they sell in the market after evaluating the 'safety-first' mechanism. The surplus wheat, pulses, and potatoes are sold in the market and in return they would buy spices, clothes, medicines and other daily necessities of life. They also barter grain with rice—the stable food in the region—from Bandipora district town against pulses and wheat. As people are engaged in multiple livelihoods, the income from other sources of such as livestock, also contributes to the family income. After securing the basic necessities of life, rest of the money would be used for the education of their children. Now as they have lost immediate on-farm and off-farm livelihoods, and have in hand the compensation amount which they were given against their dispossessed property; there is a fear how to use the money, as most of the underprivileged are not educated and have no expertise in other livelihood sectors except farming. Others claim the compensation is not enough, yet there are few who are caught in the 'what next' factor. However, the absentee landlord class, who own houses and property in the city, are seeing it as a blessing in disguise. For them all the options of using the money are available.

As a reference to the peasantry who were displaced in the other HEPs in Kashmir, the affected and displaced people from Bagliyar I, Bagliyar II, Uri I, and Uri II as well as from any other HEPs, did not see any change in their economic condition and instead become dependent on the market forces, and were turned from owners into workers.

The NHPC, on its parts, used the revenue it generated in the project construction not only in India, but to expand its bases and invest in the overseas projects. The electricity generated from Kashmir is supplied to major Indian cities, to cater to the demands of the rising capitalist class, and this in turn increases the production and income of the corporation. The corporation, which was only engaged in the HEP construction, has now diversified its investment in other sectors.

The State of Jammu and Kashmir, on the other hand, gets a meagre 12 per cent of revenue from these HEPs which it uses to either enhance its own electricity generation capacity or to purchase electricity from the northern states during the winter season when the local electricity generation goes to the minimal level. The state which is facing debt crisis and is heavily dependent on the central government's assistance to meet its necessary expenditures, is often accused by the civil society actors for letting NHPC exploit the state's natural resources, which as per local dominant discourse is believed to fix all the economic woes of the state. With external pressure from political parties and civil society groups mounting, the state government passed the Jammu and Kashmir Water Resources (Regulation and Management) Act, 2010 which allows the state to charge all the agencies which would generate the electricity for water usage. The state government believes that this legislation would help the state to generate millions of revenue, which would enable it to use the money for electricity generation. However, in reality the legislation was never implemented.

The Power of Decision-Making

One of the crucial questions about land deals in Kashmir is to answer, who gets to decide. While at the surface level it is the State that takes the land, for 'public purpose', that is, electricity generation for the 'public good'; however, at the macro level, it is the NHPC-led capital on the behest of the Indian State, which dictates the local state to facilitate land deals for HEP construction. Since 1975 when the State decided to build the HEPs, it did not have sufficient capital to do so, therefore it approached the central government to get the funding for the construction of HEPs but wished to keep its sovereign rights over the HEPs. However, the central government refused to give the State of Jammu and Kashmir sovereign rights; instead it promised to provide funding for the construction of HEPs on the equal share (CSC 2011). The central government allocated construction of HEPs to NHPC, stating the reason that the state government does not have the capacity to execute the HEPs. The state government, with limited financial capital to execute the projects, had to budge before the centre. While the centre promised to give back the power projects after the stipulated time, the state never got the projects back because of the state's inability to negotiate, persuade or pressurize NHPC to return the HEPs. The mainstream[2] politicians at the helm of affairs, often face legitimacy problem to rule the state, have to turn to the centre for their existence, therefore, they have hardly taken a strong stand to get back the power projects. Under these circumstances, NHPC with the support of the central government, together with the subservience from the local government are the main players who decide about the land acquisitions. The decisions are taken either through extra-economic coercion or with the support of local government officials who change local land records, against the benefits they get in the form of cash and kind from the corporation. Moreover, the corporation also uses absentee landlords, who because of their affiliation with the concurrent regimes, and their non-association with the land, facilitate land deals. In this process, those who are the most affected do not have a sway in the decision-making process.

Since 1975, successive state governments have failed to get back these power projects. For the separatists, these power projects, as discussed in Chapter 4, were not seen as a cause worth to fight for unless Kashmir gets

[2] Mainstream politicians are those who contest elections under Indian Constitution and show their allegiance to India. Though they are elected through a democratic process, but the dominant discourse is that they lack legitimacy to rule as they are the stooges of Indian state in Kashmir. Understanding their weaknesses, they cannot push the Government of India to transfer the power projects, as their survival lies on keeping New Delhi happy.

independence from India. This approach changed from early 2000 and the realization has come that energy sovereignty cannot be kept subservient to political sovereignty.

Nevertheless, as discussed in Chapters 1 and 6, resistance and fight for the return of power projects by the mainstream parties have not yielded any positive result. Even in the current People's Democratic Party-BJP regime which in its common minimum programme (CMP) had committed to negotiate with NHPC to transfer the projects to J&K government, but nothing concrete has been seen in the last two and a half years. NHPC has rather made it clear to the state government that it cannot transfer the projects, reflecting the fact that the power to decide lies somewhere in Delhi.

***

Land in rural Kashmir is considered to be the single most important asset which, in the context of minimal state-led social welfare, provides not only social security but social status as well. The land is collateral for the poor farmer to get a loan for a family member's sickness or a daughter's wedding. The land is given as dowry and as dower, the land is an identity for the people. The land has graveyards, churches, mosques, and temples and in turns the related associations with it. In fact, the 60-year-old conflict in Kashmir, which has consumed over 60,000 human lives, has also a dimension of a conflict over the land. While there is a larger resistance movement for political sovereignty in Kashmir, the intrusion of NHPC in the form of building dams, power projects, and residential and official quarters, has created a lot of pressure of domestic capital on people in the mountainous area of Gurez, which has in turn led to their dispossession and displacement, and has left an impact on traditional livelihoods as well as severely affected local ecology.

While the larger debate of land-grabbing in the global context is confined to external corporations, but to the grabbing of native land and sometimes water, not much attention has been paid especially on how state-owned national corporations do the same on the pretext of national/public interests. Kishanganga Power Project and previous power projects in Kashmir by NHPC present the classic case of a state corporation exploiting peripheral resources, creating depeasantization in the country-side and leaving behind dispossessed and displaced peasantry.

This book has tried to present and analyse the political processes sur-rounding land-grabbing in Kashmir. From land and water politics in South Asia, land-grabs around the world, economic and political history of land-grabs in India, land tenure changes in Kashmir, and the impact and response to the land-grabs in Gurez, this work has focused on land-grabbing in a conflict zone in light of contemporary land-grabs in the world.

Contemporary land-grabs have become a catch-all phrase for scholars, political activists, journalists and people from all shades of social, public and political space. A sizeable amount of scholarship has been produced since the land-grabbing debate surfaced in 2008 after the world food crisis. However, this scholarship was largely region and actor centred, wherein the focus was on land-grabs in Africa and Latin America, and the actors, like Gulf countries, China, India, South Korea, and corporations from other countries, were involved in these land deals. While the post 2013 scholarship on land-grabs focused across the regions, even though still dominated by Africa and Latin America, yet focused on what type of land is being grabbed and who are the investors. But the more important questions of 'how' and 'why' remained largely unaddressed, how the land was acquired and what was the process of control-grabbing, who played the role, what had been the underlying interests, positions and power relations in taking the land, supporting or facilitating such land deals, and, the question of 'why' a specific land was taken and why not the other land, have remained unaddressed along with the question regarding the purposes of taking this land. Furthermore, land-grabs in conflict zones and disputed territories remained untouched. Thus, this work is not only among the few works that have been produced in a small region focusing on the process of land-grabs but it is, so far, the only study conducted on land-grabs in a disputed and conflict-ridden territory.

This analysis of land-grabs in Kashmir started from exploring why land-grabs in this state remain unnoticed despite being one of the widely reported conflict zones in the world. In the first chapter of this book

I looked at the larger question of hydropower politics in South Asia. This was done to understand Kashmiri narratives of exploitation of their natural resources by NHPC. It looked at the question as to why Kashmiris are not given a fair share of water under IWT. It has also addressed the fact why Kashmiris feel that their economic problems emerge due to India and Pakistan's control over water resources available in Kashmir and how the economic empowerment of Kashmir is seen possible only through gaining control of these resources. In doing so I explained why and how peasantry is getting neglected in the larger narratives.

Further, the study looked at the strategies and narratives adopted by the State, corporate and elites to justify or facilitate land-grabs. Then the book worked out the strategies and motivations of different actors to support or resist the land-grabs. And finally, I elicited peasant strategies and responses to the land-grabs, and how they were able to galvanize the external support from civil society and media.

To contextualize this work, I explored the land-grabs debate across the world, the actors involved, and resistance offered in these land deals. I highlighted the role of the state in controlling these deals and how state and corporate work in tandem to control such deals. I further explained how extra-economic power is being used to mussel the voices of peasants in the lands deals.

In order to understand the phenomena of land-grabbing by the state-owned or semi-government corporations in Kashmir, I analysed land- and resources-grabs in India from the colonial period to the present times. Thus in Chapter 3, I argued that India has so far largely followed the colonial approach towards land appropriation. These acquisitions, even though done in the name of development, are far from being pro-peasant and/or pro-ecology. While this land-grab increased after 1990 when India opened its economy, it intensified after the establishment of SEZs. However, peasant atrocities at the hands of capital started coming to the fore for the first time in post independent India.

While most of the Indian states were chasing foreign capital for development in post 1990, Kashmir, a case *sui generis* in India, did not become an attraction for these investors due to the ongoing armed conflict. Nevertheless, Kashmir could not keep itself aloof from the State-corporate nexus of resource hunt. The water resources in Kashmir were seen as apt for electricity generation which would illuminate energy hungry Indian cities. The state used extra-economic and extra-judicial forces to control land in Kashmir. Therefore, it is argued that Kashmir peasants reflect different identities, especially the identity of being Kashmiri and Kashmir conflict as the core of their politics. Here the peasants not only see themselves as a part of a community and exert their rights to get their land-specific problems addressed, but they also associate themselves as core members of the larger Kashmiri community, who take part in the larger struggle—'Independence from India'. Thus, James Scott's framing of treating peasants as a monolithic community who are interesting in material interests gets negated. With this background, it is argued that land-grabs in Kashmir have to be understood in its unique political and geographic setting.

Control on private as well as common property resources by the capital, deconstructs the global notion that the absence of property rights of people over their land majorly leads to land-grabs. Land tenure security as an instrument to combat land-grabs seems too fallible. Land-grabbing of the scale reported in this study cause hardships on peasants. The negative impact of the same is borne by economic resources, culture, tradition, livelihoods, common property resources and ecology, and a deterioration of social capital.

The exploitation of natural resources, control of land and waters, however, was made possible (a) through the corporate nexus with politicians/bureaucrats to change the land records; conceal the government-corporate agreements, in lieu of cash and kind to benefit the corporation; (b) through the support of absentee landlords who also held important government positions; and (c) the continuous support to the corporation and pressurization of local government by the central government to abide by the corporation dictates. Exploitation of natural resources of Kashmir and denial of paying back a due share of electricity and compensation has marred the Kashmiri peasantry in particular and Kashmir economy in general. On the contrary, NHPC has grown over the years and become one of the biggest corporates in India, however, its investment in Kashmir in terms of the development of infrastructure, employment generation and claims of solving power crisis of the region are nowhere visible. The corporation's promises of providing 24-hour electricity to the affected areas, a scholarship to their wards, and jobs to the locals, have at the end proved just rhetoric and a means to take the land from people.

With NHPC gaining the lion's share in the prevailing arrangement, it is the State of J&K, which is losing money and resources to NHPC. The peasants, on the other hand, lost the land, houses, jobs, culture, and the values and customs related to land and natural resources.

Under these circumstances different actors involved in the Kashmir HEPs offered a varied form of resistance. Pakistan uses political, diplomatic, legal and armed resistance against these projects as they believe they violate IWT norms. On the other hand, in Kashmir there is resistance against dispossession and displacement by peasants, and resistance for compensation by the state, local political parties, civil society groups, and peasants. Some of these resistance struggles are covert and some of them are overt. However, here too, peasant struggles against the 'capital' are often engulfed by larger narratives of two the countries—India and Pakistan, about KHEP, which leads to submersion of the peasant narrative, who are the main affected actors of this HEP. No doubt people's resistance and pressure from Pakistan made India to change the KHEP design and, therefore decreased the adverse impact of the KHEP from the initial plan of displacing 25 villages to 2 villages. However, the left out two villages resisted the land-grabs and displacement, but could not succeed in front of the mighty state which acquired the land and houses. As the peasants' lost the battle against land-grabs, there was a gradual transition in the nature of peasant resistance. Resistance against land-grabs has over the years became an ordeal for compensation.

To quell peasant resistance at the ground level, the state has used the carrot and stick policy. Stringent laws are enforced in the land acquisition process. The corporation made promises to increase compensation. Bringing people into 'compensation trap', the corporation offered compensation in the form of cash, scholarships, and jobs, to make people agree to give up their land. However, the tall claims of the compensation have proved bogus. While initially jobs were provided by the corporation, however, it has been observed that as the corporation completed the construction work, these workers are laid-off, thus creating a phenomenon 'where land is needed labour is not' (Li 2011). On the other hand, while peasants are displaced to hundreds of kilometres away, a sizable chunk of their land is not acquired, which creates another phenomenon; when neither land is needed nor the labour.

Thus state did not only play a major role in dispossessing and displacing the current generation but by exploiting the natural resources, it did not pay any attention to the needs of the future generation either. What was revealed that the State not only provided the land and issued a sanction to cut down forest trees for the construction of tunnels, it also identified the land, facilitated the land-grabs, and used the force to quell the resistance against the land-grabs. However, when the land was brought under control, and peasants' resistance turned from resistance against land-grabs to resistance for compensation, the State supported this resistance, as it had already achieved its purpose of giving the possession of land to NHPC. Thus the State played a dual role; first it facilitated land-grabs, and then supported the resistance for compensation to secure their political constituency to get the 'legitimacy'. Officially, the government argues that the land has been leased out only to the NHPC and has not been given the ownership of the land. However, the fact that NHPC controlled the HEPs for decades, which not only negates the bureaucratic terminology of ownership, but also violates Article 370 of the Indian constitution, which gives special status to the region, under which only permanent residents of the region can own the land. Here Pigou reminds us of the functions and responsibilities of the State for the future generation:

> There is wide agreement that the State should protect the interests of the future generations to some degree against the effects of our irrational discounting and of our preference for ourselves over our descendants ... It is

the clear duty of Government, which is the trustee for un-born generations as well as for its present citizens, to watch over, and, if need, be, by legislative enactment, to defend, the exhaustible natural resources of the country from reckless spoliation. (Pigou 1932)

Nevertheless, it was revealed, that mostly young and village elites, fall into the 'compensation trap', while elders and women fight against dispossession and displacement. On the other hand, the state of Jammu and Kashmir and civil society groups in Kashmir, fight for compensation as well. Here I argue that resistance for compensation by the peasants is a method of resistance against the land-grabs to make the State annoyed, and tired, and therefore to give up the land acquisition process by way of demanding too much compensation which is either beyond the control/capacity of the corporation, or to settle the score with the corporation to get the maximum possible compensation. Yet the dichotomy of some people not resisting against the land but for water-grabs, has to do with the inaccessibility of the area, which remains cut off for half of the year, due to heavy snowfall, and is inaccessible to the State machinery, which leads to dependence of the people on the military. It is this very dependence on the military, the State, and exclusion from rest of the Kashmir population where these people have to offer resistance. Thus it is important to understand the question of resistance through the political structure in which it occurs.

As the peasants have been protesting against these HEPs, however, these protests have not become the part of the debate in the media, in the policy circles or academia in India. In fact peasants' resistance against the HEPs did not become a debate in Kashmir either, till late 2000, as most of the literature on Kashmir was/is focused on Kashmiri's political struggle. Therefore, the struggles by the local peasantry against the capital remained unheard and were engulfed by the larger Kashmiri 'struggle for Independence'. As relative normalcy' has returned to the valley, these 'development projects' have taken a debate and a mode of resistance in the region. This debate has further sharpened due to the fact that unemployment and underemployment in the region have sharply increased, while the key elements of ground narratives are the water resources which are exploited by India through NHPC and are believed to be the root of all the economic woes.

KHEP is not the only HEP executed by the NHPC which is leading to dispossession and displacement of the peasantry. Since its inception in 1970s NHPC run HEPs have led dispossession and displacement of thousands of people—all in the name of 'development'. This theory of development has been deconstructed by the respondents, who experienced that extraction of their resources, would yield no benefit to them. For example, the area (Gurez) which is to produce 330 MW of electricity from KHEP has to rely for electricity on kerosene generator, which provides only four hours electricity in 24 hours.

I argue that the mainstream economists and scholars view in favour of 'land acquisition for development', by the capital would bring 'development' to the recipient country is misleading. It is important here to question this perspective of looking at only economic dimensions of the land, while ignoring the indigenous people's right to land and right to move. Treating land as a commodity is grossly misleading and unjustifiable. Here it would not be out of place to highlight what Polanyi had decades earlier cautioned, that treating natural resources only through economic dimensions is a hazardous endeavour from the socio-political and cultural sustainability point of view:

> To allow the market mechanism to be the sole director of the fate of human beings and their natural environment, indeed, even of the amount and use of purchasing power, would result in the demolition of society. For the alleged commodity 'labor power' cannot be shoved about, used indiscriminately, or even left unused, without affecting also the human individual who happens to be the bearer of this peculiar commodity ... Robbed of the protective covering of cultural institutions, human beings would perish from the effects of social exposure; they would die as the victims of acute social dislocation through vice, perversion, crime, and starvation. Nature would be reduced to its elements, neighborhoods and landscapes filled, rivers polluted, military safety jeopardized, the power to produce food and raw materials destroyed. Finally, the market administration of purchasing power would periodically liquidate business enterprise, for shortages and surfeits of money would prove as disastrous to business and floods and

droughts in primitive society ... But no society could stand the effects of such a system of crude fictions even for the shortest stretch of time unless its human and natural substance as well as its business organization was protected against the ravages of this satanic mill. (Polanyi 1944: 73)

Expanding Franco et al. (2013) and Woodhouse and Ganho's (2011) arguments of linking contemporary land-grabs with water-grabbing, an argument is made that in HEPs it is important to grab water and land together to generate electricity. Therefore, in Kashmir, while the land of the peasant was taken to build dams and power projects, the water of the river, which would be used by the local rural community for drinking, washing, and irrigation of the field is now diverted from its natural route, stored, and subsequently used for power generation. The land- and water-grabbing of this kind not only adversely affects the subsistence provisions of the peasant community, harming their food sovereignty by snatching their traditional livelihoods, and subjecting them to market forces, but also considerably contributes to the emergence and development of intra-community divide. The construction of tunnels for HEPs in the forests has caused the destruction of lush green trees leading to 'privatization and commoditization of nature'.

This work mostly focused on the political processes of land-grabbing, its impacts and the responses of actors to land-grabbing. It stressed on the point that understanding the political processes of land-grabbing, the questions of resistance, narratives, and overall land politics in the fragile states, such as the conflict hit region of Kashmir, needs an entirely new framework, which theories about land-grabbing in normal regions do not offer.

This work tried to explain some of the major dimensions of land politics in Kashmir. By doing so it explained how processes and impacts of land-grab in disputed and conflict regions are different than the land-grabs that are taking place in other countries and regions. I also explained how hydropower politics is leading to resources extractivism, depeasantization, *deagrarianization*, dispossession, and displacement; and the problems associated with them were highlighted. Importantly, by bringing in perspectives of different actors on the land-grabs, this work addresses the tensions between developmentalism, environmentalism, and national interest on the one hand, and universal rights, national sovereignty, subnational identity, and resistance surrounding these grabs on the other hand.

At the completion of this work I have probably more questions about the land and water politics than I had when I started writing this book. I believe further studies could look at the questions regarding the future of the peasantry and agriculture in the era of control and diversion of water resources in Kashmir, the linkages of capital with Kashmir's capital, the Indian capital and the external capital in the land-grabs debate. While this research lays the foundation of that path, however, more deep and specific questions need to be answered. The questions such as, how the control on water, land and the construction of HEPs will shape the future relations of Kashmir with India and Pakistan, and how that will affect the geopolitics of South Asia, how will the 'control' and 'exploitation' of water resources strengthen the cause for economic independence in Kashmir from both India and Pakistan, need to be answered. Last but not the least, how will these HEPs and control on waters shape the future relation between the two nuclear powers.

Until the above questions are addressed it is important to rethink if lands are being 'acquired' for development; and if they are, then for whose development. A peasant from Badwan, who I met in July 2012, explains it for us:

> NHPC wants to illuminate *Hindustan* [India]. Neither Gurez or Bandipora nor Kashmir gets the benefit of it. They say the HEP is for the development of the country ... so do we have to *sacrifice* for the *development* of India? Who cares about what we want? We are helpless; we cannot fight against an Indian Corporation and the Indian government. They are powerful. We have to just accept the fact that we will be displaced from here. (Author interview. Emphasis in original conversation)

References

Abbasi, A. 2013. 'Kishanganga Decision is a Charge Sheet against Pakistan.' *The News* (International). Available at: http://www.thenews.com.pk/Todays-News-13-27523-Kishanganga-decision-is-a-charge-sheet-against-Pakistan [Accessed on 27 December 2013].

Adnan, S. 2007. 'Departures from Everyday Resistance and Flexible Strategies of Domination: The Making and Unmaking of Peasant Mobilization in Bangladesh', *Journal of Agrarian Change* 7(2): 183–224.

———. 2011. 'Resistance to Accumulation by Dispossession in the Context of Neoliberal Capitalism and Globalization: Struggles for Defending and Gaining Land Rights by the Poor Peasantry in the Noakhali Chars of Bangladesh'. Paper presented at 'International Conference on Global Land Grabbing', Cornell University, 6–8 April.

———. 2014. 'Panel Discussion on Comparative Land Issues in Ethnocratic Regimes: An Agenda for Research'. At 'International Conference on State Grabs of Tamil Land in the Island of Sri Lanka', 31 January–2 February.

Available at: http://tamilsforum.co.uk/wp-content/uploads/2014/05/Land-Grab-Conference-Report.pdf [Accessed on 23 June 2014].

Agamben, G. 2005. *State of Exception*. Chicago: The University of Chicago Press.

Ahluwalia, M.S. 1994. 'Commentary on India's Reform', *Journal of Business* 29(1): 17.

Ajmal, S. 2012a. 'HCC Converts Agricultural Land into Mechanical Stores'. *Greater Kashmir* (Srinagar). Available at: http://www.greaterkashmir. com/news/2012/Feb/5/-hcc-converts-agricultural-land-into-mechanical-stores—36.asp [Accessed on 15 March 2012].

———. 2012b. 'Bandipora up in Arms against HCC "noncompliance": Menacing Pollution Levels at Kishenganga Construction Site Alarms Locals'. *Greater Kashmir* (Srinagar) Available at: http://www.greaterkashmir.com/ news/2012/Dec/29/bandipora-up-in-arms-against-hcc-noncompliance —86.asp [Accessed on 5 January 2013].

Ali, M. 2012. 'NHPC behaving like East India Company. Time To Recover Water Usage Charges From All Power Corporations: Taj'. *Greater Kashmir* (Srinagar). Available at: http://www.greaterkashmir.com/news/2011/Jun/6/-nhpc-behaving-like-east-india-company—34.asp [Accessed on 25 June 2011].

Aljazeera. 2011. 'Counting the Cost. Land Grabs: Threat or the Opportunity?' Available at: http://www.aljazeera.com/programmes/countingthecost/2011/ 10/20111015124829861118.html [Accessed on 17 October 2011].

Arendt, Hannah. 1970. *On Violence*. San Diego: Harcout Brace Jovanich.

Aziz, J. 2010. 'Economic History of Modern Kashmir with Special Reference to Agriculture 1947–1989'. Unpublished PhD. Post Graduate Department of History, University of Kashmir.

Baka, J. 2011. 'Biofuels and Wastelands: Energy Policy, Land Markets and Social Inequality in South India'. International Conference on Global Land Grabbing, Land Deals Politics Initiative (LDPI), IDS Sussex.

Balakrishnan, S. 2012. 'Land Conflicts along Highways in India: A Commentary on India's Agrarian to Industrial Transition'. Paper presented at 'International Conference on Global land Grabbing', Cornell University. 17–19 October 2012.

Ballard, R. 1991. 'Kashmir Crisis: View from Mirpur', *Economic and Political Weekly* 26(9/10): 513–17.

Bardhan, P. 1998. *The Political Economy of Development in India*, 2nd edition. New Delhi: Oxford University Press.

———. 2011. 'Challenges for a Minimum Social Democracy in India', *Economic and Political Weekly* 46(10): 39–43.

Baviskar, A. 2008. 'Contract Killings: Silicosis among Adivasi migrant Workers', *Economic and Political Weekly* 43(25).

Behera, N. 2006. *Kashmir Demystifying*. Washington DC: Brooking Institution Press.

Bendfeldt, Lennart. 2010. 'Naxalism: The Maoist Challenge to the Indian State', Henrich Boll Stiftung, India.

Bernstein, H. 2010. *Class Dynamics of Agrarian Change*. Halifax: Fernwood.

Beg, A. 1995. 'On the Way to Golden Harvests: Agricultural Reforms in Kashmir'. In *Encyclopedia of Kashmir*, Vol. 10, Suresh K. Sharma and S. R. Bakshi (eds.), pp. 7–16. New Delhi: Anmol Publications Pvt. Ltd.

Bhaduri, A. 2007. 'Alternatives in Industrialization', *Economic and Political Weekly* 42(18): 1597–1601.

Bhan M. 2014. 'Morality and Martyrdom: Dams, Dharma, and The Cultural Politics of Work in Indian-Occupied Kashmir', *Biography* 37(1): 191–224.

Biggs and Matsaert. 2004. 'Strengthening Poverty Reduction Programs Using an Actor-Oriented Approach: Examples from Natural Resource Innovation Systems', *Agricultural Research and Extension Network (AgREN)*. Paper no. 134. Overseas Development Institute (ODI) London, UK.

Borras, S.M. and J.C. Franco 2010. 'Towards a Broader View of the Politics of Global Land Grab: Rethinking Land Issue, Reframing Resistance', ICAS working paper series No.00.

———. 2011. 'Political Dynamics of Land-grabbing in Southeast Asia: Understanding Europe's Role', Discussion Paper. Amsterdam: Transnational Institute.

———. 2012. 'A "Land Sovereignty" Alternative? Towards a Peoples' Counter Enclosure', TNI Agrarian Justice Programme Discussion Paper.

———. 2013. 'Global Land Grabbing and Political Reactions "From below"', *Third World Quarterly* 34(9): 1723–47.

Borras, S.M., J. Franco, and W. Chunyu. 2013. 'The Challenge of Global Governance of Land Grabbing: Changing International Agricultural Context and Competing Political Views and Strategies'. *Globalizations* 10(1): 00–00.

Borras, S.M., S. Gomez, C. Kay, J. Wilkinson. 2012. 'Land Grabbing and Global Capitalist Accumulation: Key Features in Latin America', *Canadian Journal of Development Studies* 33(4): 402–16.

Bose, S. 2003. *Kashmir Roots of Conflict Paths to Peace*. New Delhi: Vistaar Publication.

———. 2008. *The New Cambridge History of India. Peasant Labour and Colonial Capital: Rural Bengal since 1970*. Cambridge: Cambridge University Press.

Brass, T. 1999. *Peasants, Populism and Postmodernism: The Return of the Agrarian Myth*. London: Frank Cass.

Census of India. 2011. *Jammu and Kashmir Population and Geography*.

Cernea. 1990. 'Poverty Risks from Population Displacement in Water Resources Development', Development Discussion Paper No. 355. Harvard Institute for International Development: Harvard University.

———. 1997. 'The Risks and Reconstruction Model for Resettling Displaced Populations', *World Development* 2(10): 1569–87.

———. 2007. 'IRR: An Operational Risks Reduction Model for Population Resettlement', *Hydro Nepal: Journal of Water Energy and Environment* 1(1): 35–9.

Chatterjee, P. 1993. *The Nation and Its Fragments: Colonial and Postcolonial Histories*. Princeton: Princeton University Press.

Chunder, D. Ramesh. 1904. *India in the Victorian Age: An Economic History of the People*. Kegan Paul, Trench, Trubner and Co. Ltd.

Cohen, H. 2000. *The Present Absentees: The Palestinian Refugees in Israel since 1948*. Institute for Israeli Arab Studies: Jerusalem. (in Hebrew).

Cotula, L., S. Vermeulen, R. Leonard, and J. Keeley. 2009. 'Land Grab or Development Opportunity? Agriculture Investment and International Land deals in Africa', IIED/FAO/IFAD, London/Rome.

CSC. 2011. 'Issues Arising from the Terms and Conditions of Entrustment of HEP to the NHPC', *Report of the Cabinet Sub Committee (CSC) of Jammu and Kashmir Government*. 86–8.

Cuffaro, N. and D. Hallam. 2011. 'Land Grabbing in Developing Countries: Foreign Investors. Regulation and Code of Conduct'. Conference paper presented at 'International Conference on Global Land Grabbing 6–8.' Institute of Development Studies: University of Sussex.

Daily Times. 2013. 'Kishanganga Dam Case: ICA issues verdict in Pakistan's favour'. Available at: http://www.dailytimes.com.pk/national/22-Dec-2013/kishanganga-dam-case-ica-issues-verdict-in-pakistan-s-favour [Accessed on 28 December 2013].

Dar, Z. 2011–12. 'Power Projects in Jammu and Kashmir: Controversy Law and Justice', LIDS Working Papers. Harvard Law and International Development Society.

Das, A. 2011. 'Displacement: Indian State's War on its Own People', *Frontlines Of Revolutionary Struggle*. Available at: http://revolutionaryfrontlines. wordpress.com/2011/10/03/displacement-the-indian-state%E2%80% 99s-war-on-its-own-people/#more-19434 [Accessed on 14 October 2011].

Das, V. 1996. 'Dislocation and Rehabilitation: Defining a Field', *Economic and Political Weekly* 1(24): 1509–14.

Dash, K. 1999. 'India's International Monitory Fund Loans: Finessing Win-set Negotiations within Domestic and International Politics', *Asian Survey* 39(2): 884–907.

De Schutter, Olivier. 2011. 'How not to think of land-grabbing: three critiques of large-scale investments in farmland', *Journal of Peasant Studies* 38(2): 249–79.

Debal, K. and R. Singha. 2004. *Peasant Movements in Post-colonial India. Dynamics of Mobilization and Identity*. New Delhi: Sage Publications.

Desai, R. and H. Eckstein. 1990. 'Insurgency: The Transformation of Peasant Rebellion', *World Politics* 42(4): 441–65.

District Livestock Census 2011–12. Department of Animal Husbandry. Government of Jammu and Kashmir.

Dwivedi, R. 1997. 'Why Some People Resist and Others Do Not: Local Perceptions and Actions Over Displacement Risks on the Sardar Sarovar', Working Paper Series, No. 265. Institute of Social Studies: The Hague.

Edelman, M. 2013. 'Messy Hectares: Questions about the Epistemology of Land Grabbing Data', *The Journal of Peasant Studies* 40(3): 485–501.

Escobar, A. 1995. *Encountering Development: The Making and Unmaking of the Third World*. Princeton, New Jersey: Princeton University Press.

Fairhead, J., M. Leach, I. Scoones. 2012. 'Green Grabbing: A New Appropriation of Nature', *Journal of Peasant Studies* 39(2): 237–61.

FAO, IFAD, UNCTAD, and World Bank Group. 2010. 'Principles for Responsible Agricultural Investment that Respects Rights, Livelihoods, and Resources'. World Bank, Washington, DC. License: CC BY 3.0 IGO. Available at: https://openknowledge.worldbank.org/handle/10986/24101.

Feldman, S. and C. Geisler. 2011. 'Land grabbing in Bangladesh: In-Situ Displacement of Peasants Holdings'. Paper presented at 'International Conference on Global Land Grabbing' at Cornell University, 6–8 April.

Fischbach, M. 2003. *Records of Dispossession: Palestinian Refugee Property and the Arab Israeli Conflict*. New York: Columbia University Press.

Fletcher, R. 2010. 'What Are We Fighting For? Rethinking Resistance in a Pewenche Community in Chile', *Journal of Peasant Studies* 28(3): 36–67.

Forman and Kedar. 2004. 'From Arab Land to "Israel Lands": The Legal Dispossession of the Palestinians Displaced by Israel in the Wake of 1948', *Environment and Planning: Society and Space* 22: 809–30.

Foucault, M. 1978. *Discipline and Punish: The Birth of the Prison* (trans. A. Sheridan). New York: Vintage Books.

———. 1980. 'Two Lectures'. In *Power/Knowledge: Selected Interviews and other Writings—1972–1977*, Colin Gordon (ed.), p. 105. New York: Panthon.

Fox, Jonathan. 1993. *The Politics of Food in Mexico: State Power and Social Mobilization*. Ithaca, New York: Cornell University Press.

Franco, J., L. Mehta, G. Veldwisch. 2013. 'The Global Politics of Water Grabbing', *Third World Quarterly* 34(9): 1651–75.

Ganguly, S. 1996. 'Explaining Kashmir Insurgency', *International Security* 21(2): 76–107.

Golan, A. 2001. *Wartime Spatial Changes: Former Arab Territories within the State of Israel, 1948–1950*. Beer-Sheva: Ben-Gurion University Press (in Hebrew).

Graham, A., S. Aubry, R. Kunnemann, and S. M. Suurez (FIAN). 2010. 'Advancing African Agriculture (AAA): The Impact of Europe's Policies and Practices on African Agriculture and Food Security'. Land Grab Study, CSO Monitory.

GRAIN. 2008. The 2008 Land Grab for Food and Financial Security. Barcelona.

Greater Kashmir. 2013. 'JK Has Highest Unemployment Rate in North India: 5.94 Lakh Youth Register for Jobs'. Available at: http://www.greaterkashmir.com/news/jammu/jk-has-highest-unemployment-rate-in-north-india/141438.html [Accessed on January 2014].

Griffin, K., R.K. Azizur, I. Amy. 2002. 'Poverty and Distribution of Land', *Journal of Agrarian Change* 2(3): 279–330.

Guha, R. 1996. *A Rule of Property for Bengal: An Essay on the Idea of Permanent Settlement*. Durham and London: Duke University Press.

———. 1999. *Elementary Aspects of Peasant Insurgency in Colonial India*. Durham and London: Duke University Press.

———. 2006. *How Much Should a Person Consume? Thinking Through Environment*. New Delhi: Permanent Black.

———. 2008. *India After Gandhi: The History of the World's Largest Democracy*. New York: Harper Perennial.

Habib, I. 2013. *The Agrarian System of Mughal India: 1556–1707*. New Delhi: Oxford India Perennials Series. Third Edition.

Hall, D. 2013. *Land*. Cambridge, UK: Polity Press.

Hall, R. 2011. 'Land Grabbing in Southern Africa: The Many Faces of the Investor Rush', *Review of African Political Economy* 128: 193–214.

Hardiman, D. 2013. 'Towards a History of Non-Violence', *Economic and Political Weekly* XLVIII(23): 41–8.

Harriss, J. 2013. 'Does "Landlordism" Still Matter? Reflections on Agrarian Change in India', *Journal of Agrarian Change* 13(3): 351–64.

Harvey, D. 1998. *The Limits to Capital*. London: Verso.

———. 2003. *The New Imperialism*. Oxford: Oxford University Press.

International Fund for Agriculture Development. 2008. 'IFAD Policy on Improving Access to Land and Tenure Security'. Available at: https://www.ifad.org/documents/10180/404ee0e8-a385-4ce7-a6a8-e26142cb87ea [Accessed on 20 December 2013].

Ishfaq-ul-Hassan. 2012. 'Protest for Power Supply Claims Boy's Life in J&K', *DNA*. Available at: http://www.dnaindia.com/india/report-one-killed-two-injured-during-protests-over-power-shortage-in-j-and-k-1632409 [Accessed on 5 January 2012].

Jaleel, M. 2005. 'Their Final Battle for Survival'. *India Express*. Available at: http://expressindia.indianexpress.com/news/fullstory.php?newsid=46418 [Accessed on 19 May 2013].

Jean-Yves, G., H. Kiran, H. Brigitte. 2012. 'Mountain Poverty in the Hindu-Kush Himalayas', *Canadian Journal of Development Studies/Revue. Canadienne D'études du Development* 33(2): 250–65.

Joanne, Smith Finley. 2013. 'The Art of Symbolic Resistance: Uyghur Identities and Uyghur-Han Relations in Contemporary Xinjiang'. *Brill's Inner Asian Library*.

Jonathan, D.J. 2009. 'Negotiating Development: A Study of the Grassroots Resistance to India's 2005 Special Economic Zones Act', PhD Book. University of Florida.

Jones, J.D. 2009. *Negotiating Development: A Study of the Grassroots Resistance to India's 2005 Special Economic Zones Act*. PhD Thesis, University of Florida, US.

Kalhana R. 1979. *VI vs 24–67*. English Translation by M.A. Stein, 1: 238–41. New Delhi, India.

Kawa, Mushtaq. 2008. 'Land Rights in Rural Kashmir: A Study in Continuity and Change from Late-Sixteenth to Late-Twentieth Centuries', In *The Valley of Kashmir: The Making and Unmaking of a Composite Culture*, Aparna Rao (ed.). New Delhi: Manohar Publishers.

Kerkvliet, B. 2009. 'Everyday Politics in Peasant Societies (and Ours)', *Journal of Peasant Studies* 36: 227–43.

Kumar, A. 2011. 'The Battle for Land: Unaddressed Issues', *Economic and Political Weekly* XLVI(25).

Lahiri-Dutt, Radhika K., A. Nesar. 2012. 'Land Acquisition and Dispossession Private Coal Companies in Jharkhand', *Economic and Political weekly* XlVII(6).

Lamb, A. 1991. *Kashmir: A Disputed Legacy 1846–1990*. Pakistan: Oxford University Press.

Lasswell, H. 1958. *Politics: Who Gets What, When, How*. Cleveland OH: World Publishers.

Lawrence, W. 2002. *The Valley of Kashmir*. Srinagar: Wattan Publications.

Levien, Michael. 2011. 'The Politics of Dispossession: Theorizing India's "Land Wars"'. Paper presented at 'International Conference on Global Land Grabbing, Land Deal Politics Initiative', Institute for Development Studies, University of Sussex, 6–8 April 2011.

———. 2013. 'Regime of Dispossession: From Steel Town to Special Economic Zones', *Development and Change*, 44 (2): 381–407.

Lewis, I.M. 1985. *Social Anthropology in Perspective*. Cambridge: Cambridge University Press.

Li, T. 2011. 'Centering Labor in the Land Grab Debate', *The Journal of Peasant Studies* 38(2): 281–98.

Long, N. (ed.). 1989. 'Encounters at the Interface: A Perspective on Social Discontinuities in Rural Development', *Wageningen Studies in Sociology* 27, Wageningen: The Agricultural University.

———. 2001. *Development Sociology: Actor Perspectives*. London and New York: Routledge.

———. 2004. 'Actors, interfaces and development intervention: meanings, purposes and powers in Development intervention'. In *Actor and Activity Perspectives*, K. Tiina (ed.), University of Helsinki, Center for Activity Theory and Developmental Work Research and Institute for Development Studies.

Long, N. and A. Long (eds.). 1992. *Battlefields of Knowledge: The Interlocking of Theory and Practice in Social Research and Development*. London: Routledge.

Lund, C. 2011. 'Fragmented sovereignty: Land Reform and Dispossession in Laos'. *Journal of Peasant Studies* 38(4): 885–905.

Luster, C.T. 1980. *The Zero-Sum Society: Distribution and the Possibilities for Change*. New York: Basic Books.

Mahalingam, A. and A. Vyas. 2011. 'A Comparative Evaluation of Land Acquisition and Compensation Processes for Infrastructure Development in India', *Economic and Political Weekly* 46(33): 94–102.

Maitra, S. 2009. 'Development Induced Displacement: Issues of Compensation and Resettlement—Experiences from the Narmada Valley and Sardar Sarovar Project', *Japanese Journal of Political Science* 10(2): 191–211.

Majeed, Gulshan. 2015. 'Indus Water Treaty: Dissent and Agreement'. In *Breaking Mazes; An Anthology of Kehwa Talks on Kashmir*, Peer G.N. Suhail (ed.), pp. 119–25. Srinagar: Ali Mohammad and Sons.

Makki, F. and C. Geisler. 2011. 'Development by Dispossession: Land Grabbing as New Enclosures in Contemporary Ethiopia'. Paper presented at 'International Conference on Global Land Grabbing, Land Deal Politics Initiative', Institute for Development Studies, University of Sussex.

Manikumar, K.A. 2003. *A Colonial Economy in the Great Depression, Madras (1929–1937)*. Hyderabad: Orient Blackswan.

Manor, J. 1987. 'Tried, then Abandoned: Economic Liberalization in India', *IDS Bulletin* 18(4): 39–44.

Maqbool, M. 2011. 'Submerging a Culture', *Kashmir Life* 03(18).

Maqbool, U. 2012. 'In NHPC Projects, No Vacancy at Top for JK Residents: State Subjects Engaged to Perform Menial Jobs Only'. *Greater Kashmir* (Srinagar), Available at: http://www.greaterkashmir.com/news/2012/May/30/in-nhpc-projects-no-vacancy-at-top-for-jk-residents-94.asp [Accessed on 26 January 2013].

Margulis, E.M., M.K. Nora, S.M. Borras Jr., 2013. 'Land Grabbing and Global Governance: Critical Perspectives', *Globalizations* 10(1): 1–23.

Mathur, H.M. 1998. 'Impoverishment Risk Model and Its Use as a Planning Tool'. In *Development Projects and Impoverishment Risks: Resettlement Project-affected People in India*, H.M. Mathur and D. Marsden (eds), pp. 67–8. New Delhi: Oxford University Press.

———. 2008. 'Introduction and Overview'. In *India Social Development Report 2008: Development and Displacement*, H.M. Mathur (ed.), pp. 3–13. New Delhi: Council for Social Development and Oxford University Press.

Marx, K. 1976. *Capital*. Volume I. New York: Vintage.

McAdams, D.P. 2006. *The Redemptive Self: Stories Americans Live By*. New York: Oxford University Press.

Mehta, L., G. Veldwisch, and J. Franco. 2012. 'Introduction to the Special Issue: Water Grabbing? Focus on the (re)appropriation of finite Water Resources', *Water Alternatives* 5(2): 193–207.

Mishra, K. 2011. 'Behind Dispossession: State Land Grabbing and Agrarian Change in Rural Orissa.' Conference paper presented at 'International Conference on Global Land Grabbing', Institute of Development Studies, University of Sussex.

Mooij, J. 2003. 'Smart Governance? Politics in the Policy Process in Andhra Pradesh, India', Working Paper 228. ODI London, UK.

Mujumder, S. 2010. 'The Nano Controversy: Peasant Identities the Land Question and Neoliberal Industrialization in Marxist West Bengal, India', *Journal of Emerging Knowledge on Emerging Markets* 2(5): 41–66.

Mukherjee, M. 2004. *Peasant's in India's Non-Violent Revolution: Practice and Theory*. Sage Series in Modern Indian History. New Delhi: Sage Publications.

Nayak, Arun. 2015. 'Development Induced Displacement in Arms Conflicts in Bangladesh', *Conflict Studies Quarterly* 11(4): 3–23.

Neef, Andreas and Jane Singer. 2015. 'Development-Induced Displacement in Asia: Conflicts, Risks, and Resilience', *Development in Practice* 25(5): 601–11.

Neumann, W.L. 2003. *Social Research Methods: Qualitative and Quantitative Approaches*, 5th Edition. Boston USA: Aliyn and Bacon.

Nielsen, K.B. 2010. 'Contesting India's development/Industrialization, Land Acquisition and Protest in West Bengal', *Forum for Development Studies* 37(2): 145–70.

Noronha, S. 2007. 'Military Intervention and Secession in South Asia: The Cases of Bangladesh, Sri Lanka, Kashmir, and Punjab', Library of Congress Cataloging-in-Publication Data.

NRLD. 2016. Dams of National Importance. Available at: http://www.cwc.nic.in/main/downloads/National%20Register%20of%20Large%20Dams%202009.pdf [Accessed on 24 May 2013].

Nyari, B. 2008. 'Biofuel Land Grabbing in Northern Ghana.' Available at: http://biofuelwatch.org.uk/docs/biofuels_ghana.pdf [Accessed on 13 April 2003].

O'Brien and Li Lianjiang. 2006. *Rightful Resistance in Rural China*. Cambridge University Press.

O'Brien, K.J. 2013. 'Rightful Resistance Revisited', *The Journal of Peasant Studies* 40(6): 1051–62.

Ortner, S.B. 1995. 'Resistance and the Problem of Ethnographic Refusal', *Comparative Studies in Society and History* 37(1): 173–93.

Oxfam. 2011. 'Land and Power: The Growing Scandal Surrounding the New Wave of Investments in Land'. Available at: http://www. oxfam.org/sites/ www.oxfam.org/files/bp151-land-power-rightsacquisitions-220911-en.pdf. [Accessed on 19 August 2013].

———. 2013. 'Poor Governance, Good Business: How land investors target countries with weak governance'. Available at: http://policy-practice.oxfam. org.uk/publications/poor-governance-good-business-how-land-investors-target-countries-with-weak-gov-268413 [Accessed on 24 November 2013].

Oya, C. 2013. 'Methodological Reflections on "Land" Databases and the "Land Grab" Literature "Rush"', *The Journal of Peasant Studies* 40(3): 503–20.

Parvaiz, A. 2011. 'Kashmiris Hail Hague Stay on Dam', *IPS News*. Available at: http://ipsnews.net/news.asp?idnews=105254 [Accessed on 29 February 2013].

Parasuraman, S. 1999. *The Development Dilemma: Displacement in India*. New York: St. Martin's Press.

Parry, J. and C. Struempell. 2008. 'On the Desecration of Nehru's "Temples": Bhilai and Rourkela Compared', *Economic and Political Weekly* 43(19): 47–57.

Parry, J. 1999. 'Two Cheers for Reservations: The Satnamis and the Steel Plant.' In *Institutions and Inequalities: Essays in Honour of Andre Beteille*, R. Guha and J. Parry (eds.), pp. 128–69. New Delhi: Oxford University Press.

Peer, N. and J. Ye. 2015. 'Of Militarization, Counter-insurgency and Land Grabs in Kashmir', *Economic and Political Weekly* 50: 46–7.

Peretz, D. 1958. *Israel and the Palestine Arabs*. Washington, DC: Middle East Institute.

Pigou, A.C. 1932. *The Economics of Welfare: Volume 1*, 4th edition. London: Macmillan.

Polanyi, K. 1944. *The Great Transformation: the Political and Economic Origins of our Time*. Boston, MA: Beason Press.

Popkin, S. 1979. *The Rational Peasant: The Political Economy of Rural Society in Vietnam*. Berkeley: University of California Press.

Puri, B. 1981. *Triumph and Tragedy of Indian Federalisation*. Appendix 'A'. New Delhi: Sterling Publishers Pvt. Ltd.

Rai, M. 2004. *Hindu Rulers, Muslim Subjects*. New Delhi: Permanent Black.

Randle, M. 1994. *Civil Resistance*. London: Fontana.

Rasool, P.G. 2013. *Maslai Kashmir Ki Tareekhi Asliyat*. Srinagar: Ali Mohammad and Sons.

Rasool, T. 2011. 'Villagers stall Kishanganga project work: Demand employment; CM to take up issue with PM.' *Greater Kashmir* (Srinagar). Available at: http://greaterkashmir.com/news/2011/Jul/26/villagers-stall-kishanganga-project-work-41.asp&Title= [Accessed on 16 June 2013].

Richard, V. 2007. *How Countries Compete. Strategy, Structure, and Government in the Global Economy.* Boston, MA: Harvard Business School Press.

Roy, Arundhati. 2010. 'Walking with the Comrades', *Outlook*. Available at: https://www.outlookindia.com/magazine/story/walking-with-the-comrades/264738. [Accessed on 20 April 2012].

———. 2012. 'Capitalism: A Ghost Story', *Outlook*. Available at: http://www.outlookindia.com/article.aspx?280234 [Accessed on 11 November 2016].

Roy, S. 2007. *Beyond Belief: India and the Politics of Post-Colonial Nationalism.* Durham, NC: Duke University Press.

Rulli, M.C., A. Saviori, and D'Odorico. 2013. 'Global Land and Water Grabbing', *Proceedings of the National Academy of Sciences* 110(3): 892–97.

Sachs, J. and A. Warner. 1997 (revised). 'Natural Resource Abundance and Economic Growth'. National Bureau of Economic Research, Working paper No. 5398. Cambridge, MA.

Saleem, S. 2012. 'Kishanganga Project bares fangs: Thousands of trout fish found dead in Bandipora, Fisheries Department blames HCC'. *Rising Kashmir* (Srinagar). Available at: http://www.risingkashmir.in/news/kishen-ganga-project-bares-fangs-38839.aspx [Accessed on 18 November 2013].

Salih, R. and Richter-Devroe Sophie. 2014. 'Cultures of Resistance in Palestine and Beyond: On the Politics of Art, Aesthetics, and Affect'. *Arab Studies Journal* XXII(1): 8–28.

Sampat, P. 2010. 'Special Economic Zones in India: Reconfiguring Displacement in a Neoliberal Order?', *City & Society* 22: 166–82.

Sara, S. and W. Wendy. 2011. 'Contemporary Land-grabs and Their Alternatives in Americas'. Paper presented at 'International Conference on Global Land Grabbing 6–8', Institute of Development Studies, University of Sussex, 6–8 April.

Schneider, AE. 2011. 'What Shall We Do without Our Land? Land Grabs and Resistance in Rural Cambodia'. Paper presented at 'International Conference on Global Land Grabbing', Land Deal Politics Initiative'. Institute for Development Studies, University of Sussex.'

Schofield, V. 2003. *Kashmir in Conflict: India, Pakistan and the Unending War.* New edition. New York: L.B. Tauris.

Scott, J. 1976. *The Moral Economy of the Peasant: Rebellion and Subsistence in Southeast Asia*. New Haven and London: Yale University Press.

———. 1985. *Weapons of the Weak: Everyday Forms of Peasant Resistance*. New Haven: Yale University Press.

———. 1998. 'Freedom and Freehold: Space, People and State Simplification in Southeast Asia.' In *Asian Freedoms: The Idea of Freedom in East and Southeast Asia*, K. David and R. Anthony (eds.), pp. 37–64. Cambridge: Cambridge University Press.

———. 2010. *The Art of Not Being Governed: An Anarchist History of Upland Southeast Asia*. New Haven: Yale University Press.

Scudder, T. 1991. 'Development-induced Relocation and Refugee Studies: 37 Years of Change and Continuity among Zambia's Gwembe Tonga', *Journal of Refugee Studies*, Vol. 6.

Sen, A. 1999. *Development as Freedom*. Oxford: Oxford University Press.

Sérgio, S., and P.L. Sergio. 2011. 'Agrarian Structure, Foreign Investment in Land and Land Prices in Brazil', *The Journal of Peasant Studies* 39: 3–4, 873–98.

Seymour, S. 2006. *Resistance: Anthropological Theory* 6: 303–21.

Shabir, A., A. Farhet, H. Sajad, M. Ghani, F. Matoo, G. Zafar. (nd) Livelihood Facets in Gurez Valley: Status, Issues and Strategies. Sher-e-Kashmir University of Agricultural Sciences & Technology of Kashmir.

Sing, S. 1997. *Taming the Waters*. New Delhi: Oxford University Press.

Sundar, Nandini. 2007. *Subalterns and Sovereigns: An Anthropological History of Bastar, 1954–2006*. New Delhi: Oxford University Press.

Terminski, B. 2013. 'Development-induced Displacement and Resettlement: Social Problem and Human Rights Issue', Research Paper No. 9. Geneva.

Tiwari, R. 2013. 'India Wins Kishanganga Case at The Hague Court', *The Indian Express*. Available at: http://www.indianexpress.com/news/india-wins-kis-hanganga-case-at-the-hague-court/1076239/0 [Accessed on 15 December 2013].

Tribune. 2013. 'Litigation Has Gone Beyond Reach of Poor Man: SC'. Available at: http://www.tribuneindia.com/2013/20130826/nation.htm. [Accessed on April 2013].

Turton, Andrew. 1986. 'Patrolling the Middle Ground: Methodological Perspectives on "Everyday Peasant Resistance"', *Journal of Peasant Studies* 13(2): 36–48.

Tyagi, Vinay, Mayank Mishra, Aishwarya Singh. 2007. 'An Assessment of Indo-China Special Economic Zones', *Delhi Business Review* 8(1): 41–53.

Van Rooij, B., A. Lora-Wainwright, Y. Wu, Y. Zhang. 2012. 'The Compensation Trap: The Limits of Community-based Pollution Regulation in China', *Pace Environmental Law Review* 29(3): 701–45.

Vandana, A. 2008. *Discourses of Power and Resistance in Water Policy Process of New Delhi, India*. PhD. Book.

Veltmeyer, Henry. 2013. 'The New Extractivsim: An Economic Model for Inclusive Development or the New Imperialism?' Paper presented at 'COHD SEMINAR SERIES-Critical Issues in Agrarian and Development Studies' (CIADS) No. 1 (Total No. 25).

Vietor, R. 2007. *How Countries Compete. Strategy, Structure, and Government in the Global Economy*. Boston, MA: Harvard Business School Press.

Visser, O. and M. Spoor. 2011. 'Land Grabbing in Post-Soviet Eurasia: The World's Agricultural Land Reserves at Stake', *Journal of Peasant Studies* 38(2): 299–323.

Wade, R. 1985. 'The Market for Public Office: Why the Indian State is not Better at Development', *World Development* 13(4): 467–97.

Walker, K.L.M. 2008. 'From Covert to Overt: Everyday Peasant Politics in China and the Implications for Transnational Agrarian Movements', *Journal of Agrarian Change* 8(2–3): 462–88.

Wasim, A. 2013. 'Kishanganga Dispute with India: Govt Criticised in Senate over Hague Court Verdict', *Dawn News*. Available at: http://www.dawn.com/news/788927/kishanganga-dispute-with-india-govt-criticised-in-senate-over-hague-court-verdict [Accessed on 17 December 2013].

Wells, A. 2007. 'Imperial Hegemony and Colonial Labour', *Rethinking Marxism* 19(2): 180–99.

Williamson, John. 1990. 'What Washington means by policy reform'. In *Latin American Adjustment: How Much Has Happened?*, John Williamson (ed.). Washington: Institute for International Economics.

Wirsing, R.G. and C. Jasparro. 2006. 'Spotlight on Indus River Diplomacy: India, Pakistan, and the Baglihar Dam Dispute', Asia-Pacific Center for Security Studies. Available at: http://www.apcss.org/Publications/APSSS/IndusRiverDiplomacy.Wirsing.Jasparro.pdf.

White, Ben, Borras Jr., Hall Ruth, Scoones Ian & Wolford Wendy. 2012. 'The New Enclosures: Critical Perspectives on Corporate Land Deals', *Journal of Peasant Studies* 39(3–4): 619–47.

Whitehead, J. and John Locke. 2011. 'Accumulation by Dispossession and the Governance of Colonial India', *Journal of Contemporary Asia* 42(1): 1–21.

Wolf, E. 1969. *Peasants Wars of Twentieth Century*. New York: Harper & Row.

Woodhouse, P. and A.S. Ganho. 2011. 'Is Water the Hidden Agenda of Agricultural Land Acquisition in Sub-Saharan Africa?' Paper presented at the 'International Conference on Global Land Grabbing'; 6–8 April 2011; University of Sussex, UK. Available at: http://www.future-agricultures.org/papers-and-presentations/cat_view/1551-global-land-grab/1552-conference-papers?start=10: Future Agricultures Consortium; 2011.

World Bank. 2010. 'Rising Global Interest in Farmland: Can It Yield Sustainable and Equitable Results?', Washington, DC: World Bank.

Yaseen, Faisul. 2016. 'Loss to Jammu Kashmir: Rs 194320000000: NHPC deprived JK of this money in 14 years'. *Rising Kashmir*. Available at: http://www.risingkashmir.com/news/loss-to-jammu-kashmir-rs-194320000000/. [Accessed on July 2016].

Zargar, Ab. Majid. 2011. 'The dubious role of NHPC in J&K'. *Rising Kashmir*. Available at http://www.risingkashmir.com/news/the-dubious-role-of-nhpc-in-jk-18293.aspx. [Accessed on 22 January 2013].

Zulu, L., and S. Wilson. 2012. 'Whose Minerals, Whose Development? Rhetoric and Reality in Post-Conflict Sierra Leone', *Development and Change* 43(5): 1103–31.

Index

About the Author

Peer Ghulam Nabi Suhail is a Kashmir-based scholar, writer, commentator, policy analyst, and development expert. A fellow at the International Poverty Reduction Centre at Beijing, China, Suhail earned his PhD in International Development Studies from the College of Humanities and Development Studies, China Agricultural University, and a master's degree in public policy from the School of Public Policy and Management, Tsinghua University, China. He also holds a master's degree in Indian history from the University of Kashmir. His scholarly work includes projects and publications on political economy of development, agrarian political economy, governing globalization, land and water politics, microfinance, disaster and development, military led development, and third sector governance. He has edited, *Breaking Mazes: An Anthology of KehwaTalks on Kashmir* (Ali Mohammad and Sons, 2015) and has successfully organized a discussion platform called 'Kashmir Social Entrepreneurship Circle 2006–08'.

In 2008 Suhail founded Kashmir's first, and so far, the only public policy think-tank, Centre for Research and Development Policy (CRDP).